NOT YOUR MOTHER'S

Retirement

*To Dorian Mintzer, for her invaluable wisdom,
insights, and recommendations*

Published by Sellers Publishing, Inc.

Copyright © 2014 Sellers Publishing, Inc.

All rights reserved.

Credits: page 224

Sellers Publishing, Inc.
161 John Roberts Road, South Portland, Maine 04106
Visit our Web site: www.sellerspublishing.com • E-mail: rsp@rsvp.com

Design by Jen Adam (jenadam.com)

ISBN 13: 978-1-4162-4518-6
e-ISBN: 978-1-4162-4525-4
Library of Congress Control Number: 2013945239

The ideas and suggestions expressed in this book are not intended
as a substitute for the financial or medical advice of your financial
adviser or trained health professional. All matters regarding your
health require medical supervision. Where appropriate, consult your
physician before adopting the suggestions in this book, as well as
about any condition that may require diagnosis or medical attention.
The publisher disclaims any liability arising directly or
indirectly from the use of the book.

10 9 8 7 6 5 4 3 2 1

Printed in the United States of America.

Not Your Mother's Retirement

Secrets for Today's Women to Live Fully During the Best Years of Life

Expert contributors provide advice on housing, work,
financial planning, travel, volunteering, lifelong learning,
caregiving, spirituality, being single, health,
and staying active in retirement.

Edited by Mark Evan Chimsky

SELLERS
PUBLISHING

CONTENTS

INTRODUCTION

When I was in the early stages of developing *Not Your Mother's Retirement*, one glaring fact caught my attention: *Huffington Post* reported that according to research by the Transamerica Center for Retirement Studies, "only 29 percent of women have made saving for retirement their top financial priority." Without starting to plan years ahead of time, retirement can creep up on us and all of a sudden it's too late to start saving enough or making well-thought-out decisions in advance about the future. Suddenly, the future has become the present. Most women say that they are too busy caring for others — kids, spouses, partners — and just trying to balance (or as my friend Aliza Sherman says, "juggle") work and home life to find time to think about their own needs. As Catherine Collinson, president of the Transamerica Center for Retirement Studies, told *Huffington Post*: "As women, we're so busy with our priorities day to day — whether they be family or work or some form of caregiving — that women are shortchanging themselves when it comes to planning for the long term." We could learn a lesson from flight attendants, who, when they're demonstrating the deployment of oxygen masks in an emergency, tell us: put one on yourself first, or you won't be able to help your loved ones.

When it comes to retirement planning, you don't need an emergency to start putting your own needs front and center. You do need time. And that's the reason for this book. Our aim is to provide valuable advice and recommendations to women in their 40s and 50s so that they can take action when it can still make a big difference. My hope is that you've bought this book for that very purpose: to jump-start the retirement-planning process so you can have the kind of retirement you really want. And the reassuring message here is that you *can* make that happen.

And before I go farther, a word about "the word" — *retirement*. I know, for many it just doesn't apply any longer. Certainly, more and more of you are not retiring from the workforce, but are choosing to pursue a different kind of job or career path, using conscious intention to find work that is personally meaningful and fulfilling. Nowadays, the entire concept of retirement is radically different than it was in the past. That's why I'm calling this book *Not Your Mother's Retirement*. Choose another word that feels more appropriate to you. Redefine it, reinvent it, retire "retirement," forge a new vision (and word) for your next chapter. Whatever you call it, I like to say that the later years are no longer just about "recreation" but about "*re*-creation." It's your turn to identify what you want to do with your life and who you want to be.

Recent surveys reveal that one of the things that women fear most about retirement is not being able to make ends meet — having to live on the edge, or even outliving their money. A 2013 study on "Women, Money, and Power" from the Allianz Life Insurance Company of North America revealed that 49 percent of women worry about "becoming a bag lady" in their retirement years. (What's interesting is that 60 percent of the women concerned about this were the "primary breadwinners" of their households.) The image of the bag-lady retirement apparently looms large, a nightmare that causes 4:00-in-the-morning sleeplessness. So, why does this specter haunt women in increasing numbers? Researchers say it's because the safety nets are becoming fewer and fewer — and also because a lack of preparation leads to fear, and worries of worst-case scenarios can trump action. But you know that doesn't have to be the case. That's why you took a proactive step and are seeing what the 20 experts in this book have to say.

And what a collection of contributors this book contains! As I developed this project, I set the bar high — I wanted to include experts in their fields who would provide practical tools and information that could help women to create a successful retirement for themselves down the road. I plowed through studies and Web sites and talked to a wide range of women to find out what was of uppermost concern, and then, based on this research, I mapped out ten essential areas I wanted to address: housing, finances, work, travel, health, caregiving, volunteering, education, spirituality, and living solo. And then I went about finding writers who could provide guidance on how to make all these aspects of one's later years as rewarding as possible.

In *Not Your Mother's Retirement,* you'll find illuminating essays on housing options by the award-winning writer Sally Abrahms and Kathryn McCamant, the architect who introduced the concept of "cohousing" to the United States. M. Cindy Hounsell, president of the Women's Institute for a Secure Retirement (WISER), and Julie Jason, a respected adviser in retirement investing, provide essays that will help you hone your financial literacy and take action to save wisely for your retirement.

Read the essays by Marci Alboher, the expert on encore careers, and Nancy Collamer, a prominent career coach, to learn about pursuing a career with purpose in your later years. And for those who'd rather play than work, you'll enjoy the information-packed essays on unique travel opportunities that won't break your budget, by travel mavens Akaisha Kaderli and Nancy Thompson.

And when you're done exploring the world, think about expanding your horizons in other ways, such as taking lifelong-learning courses. Kali Lightfoot, executive director of the National Resource Center for the Osher Lifelong Learning Institutes (OLLI), and Nancy Merz Nordstrom, a proponent of "learning later," offer a smorgasbord of ideas and topics that will hopefully intrigue and inspire you — either to take a course or teach one!

For those of you who, like my friend Lenora, say that what scares you most about retirement is "not being able to be of use; feeling like I won't have a purpose," the essays on volunteering by Shirley Sagawa, a pioneer of the volunteer movement, and Dawn Angelo, a volunteer-advocate, will offer you a wealth of fascinating ideas to consider.

Statistics show that many women will become caregivers in retirement — either of partners or parents or both. To prepare you to find ways to help others while also paying attention to your own well-being, read the enlightening essay by Paula Solomon, a noted coach and family caregiver herself.

If you want to keep active in retirement, there are practical essays by Elizabeth O'Brien, a savvy MarketWatch.com columnist on retirement, and Moira Lanier, a popular fitness expert, that will show you how to get in shape now so that you have a healthy retirement later.

One aspect that may nourish and sustain you as you build your diversified "life portfolio" is your own sense of spirituality. Rev. Pat Hoertdoerfer, an experienced educator and Unitarian Universalist minister, offers a profoundly moving look at the spiritual stages of the retirement process and how your own individual faith can help you through them. Amy Wood, an award-winning psychologist, weighs in on the importance of listening to your inner compass.

In addition, the book includes a useful essay on how to enjoy retirement while being single by Sara Zeff Geber, an esteemed life-planning coach. There are also essays that cover general topics of interest — from a wide-ranging overview of retirement by Dorian Mintzer, a leading retirement expert, to a look at the benefits of having a "circle of trust" by Suzanne Braun Levine, one of the foremost authorities on women.

A note about the format of the book. One of the pieces of good news from the research by the Transamerica Center for Retirement Studies is that "women are eager to do better" when it comes to retirement planning. They are "more likely than men to desire a good starting point and easy-to-understand educational materials." Bearing that in mind, we sought a user-friendly design for busy women who wanted access to good information but who didn't want to wade through a lot of dense text to get it. I want to thank the wise team at Sellers who were instrumental in proposing this unique design concept: Publishing Director Robin Haywood, Managing Editor Mary Baldwin, and the sales group: Cynthia Kurtz, Diana Kipp, and Jo Ann Van Reenen. We took a magazine approach, encouraging our contributors to use checklists, bullet points, callouts, anecdotes, resources, and action steps. I was impressed by the way they delivered lively, highly readable essays that distilled important, sometimes complex information in an accessible way. Helping to make this concept a reality were designer Jen Adam and production editor Charlotte Cromwell — my appreciation to both of them for their skill and creativity.

And last but certainly not least, I want to express my deep gratitude to the 20 contributors to this book, who so generously provided their essays on a pro-bono basis so that we could donate all the royalties from the sale of *Not Your Mother's Retirement* to cancer research and prevention. Their insights, advice, and expertise will hopefully help you to plan confidently and successfully so that your retirement/rewirement/redefinement and re-creation years are rich with possibilities.

Mark Evan Chimsky
January 2014

ACHIEVING FINANCIAL INDEPENDENCE:

How Women Can Create Retirement Wealth

BY JULIE JASON

A trusted voice in retirement investing offers an important message about financial literacy: There is *always* something you can do to improve your financial situation.

Over the last 20 years, money manager and lawyer Julie Jason has established herself as an expert in retirement investing, a special focus of her firm, Jackson, Grant Investment Advisers, Inc., of Stamford, Connecticut. She is the author of two highly acclaimed books on the subject, *The AARP® Retirement Survival Guide* and *Managing Retirement Wealth*, both winners of the prestigious EIFLE Award for Excellence in Financial Literacy Education. Visit juliejason.com or jacksongrantus.com.

CREATING RETIREMENT WEALTH

Wisdom and knowledge grow with experience. With hindsight, I'm sure you'll agree you would have done some things in your life differently if you only knew what you know now. When it comes to finances, the future is easily set in motion by what you do today. No matter what your age or circumstances, I assure you that you can take action today that will help you achieve financial independence for the rest of your life.

TAKING THE LONG VIEW

Financial security is within every person's reach, because wealth is a function of time and math. The sooner you start investing properly, the more money you will have to secure your financial independence. You don't have to be a genius or a market wizard. You only have to take advantage of the power of compounding. Think of compounding as interest on interest. The more time you have, the longer you earn interest on interest. It's the math behind wealth creation. No matter your age, you can still put *time* to work for you — and that mathematical phenomenon is what makes women wealthy.

> "Start by studying your own finances and look for small ways to improve your situation."

HOW TO BECOME FINANCIALLY CONFIDENT

Survey data concludes that women are not confident making financial decisions. That may sound like a problem, but let me assure you it isn't. Behavioral economists have determined that overconfidence is one reason behind bad financial results. It's better to know that you don't know enough, as long as that feeling puts you on a course of discovery.

The fact is, it does take some work to learn how to do anything, from baking a cake to mowing the lawn, to changing a lightbulb, and even brushing your teeth. There is a first time for everything. Why should women resist learning about finances when it's so important to their personal welfare? Could math anxiety be the culprit? Or the feeling that there is too much to learn?

Become Financially Literate

Understand these key definitions, and you'll soon be on your way to making knowledgeable financial decisions.

- ▶ **Compounding:** The power of compounding creates retirement wealth.

- ▶ **Knowledge:** You don't have to be a market wizard to understand how the principle of compounding can be put to work for you.

- ▶ **Markets:** The financial markets are uncertain and will always be uncertain.

- ▶ **Bubbles:** If the stock market looks like a sure bet, as it did during the Internet bubble, it's time to be cautious.

- ▶ **Loss:** Studies of investors show that people lose money by selling at the wrong time.

- ▶ **Risk:** Risk-assessment questionnaires are useless. No one wants to lose money.

- ▶ **Expectations:** Manage expectations — in the ideal world, investors would expect what they can't have: high returns without any risk. All investing involves risk; your job is to understand the risk of every investment before taking it on.

- ▶ **Returns:** Your investment returns will largely depend on market trends.

- ▶ **Asset allocation:** Studies show that allocations between stocks, bonds, and cash influence results.

- ▶ **Purchasing power:** Over time, inflation increases the costs.

- ▶ **Taxes:** Taxes negatively impact returns.

- ▶ **Safe investments:** "Safety" means different things to different people.

- ▶ **Under the mattress:** Money under the mattress may feel safe, but take it out and it will buy less.

- ▶ **Cash flows:** Successful retirees calculate their personal cash flows — money coming into the household vs. money leaving the household to pay bills.

▶ **Advisers:** When you hire an attorney, accountant, or a financial adviser, you are the boss.

▶ **Time:** Time is on your side. It is an investor's ally.

▶ **Investors:** The job of the investor is to put money to work prudently, effectively, and efficiently.

▶ **Get personal:** Study your own situation to decide what's best for you.

▶ **401(k):** A retirement plan at work that allows you to invest through regular payroll deductions ("salary deferrals"). Investments grow tax-deferred (tax-free if you have a Roth IRA). For more information on 401(k)s, search the IRS Web site at irs.gov.

▶ **Behavioral economics:** The study of emotions and other nonfinancial factors that influence how we make financial decisions.

▶ **Bonds:** Bonds represent a creditor's rights and a debtor's obligations. Companies issue bonds when they want to raise capital for different business purposes. When you buy a bond, you are lending money to the company. In return, the company promises to pay you back at a certain date in the future when the bond "matures," plus interest during the time you own the bond.

▶ **Mutual funds:** An investment vehicle that offers investors a way to hire a professional portfolio manager at amounts that are lower than otherwise possible. For example, you may need $10 million to work with a manager directly, or you can buy the same manager's mutual fund with only $2,000.

▶ **Roth IRA:** An individual retirement account that you set up yourself through a brokerage firm, mutual fund company, or bank. The nice thing about a Roth is that withdrawals are not taxed (in contrast to a "traditional" IRA). Learn more about both Roth and traditional IRAs online at irs.gov.

▶ **Roth IRA loophole:** Some people make more than permitted by IRS rules to qualify to contribute to a Roth IRA for themselves. However, anyone earning any amount can convert an existing IRA to a Roth IRA. Conversions usually mean paying taxes on the amount converted, but not always. To see how this applies to you, read IRS Publication 590, which is updated each year and that you can find online at irs.gov, or e-mail me at: readers@juliejason.com.

- **S&P 500 Index:** A representation of the U.S. stock market's price movement, which is published by Standard & Poor's Corporation. The Index is made up of 500 widely held common stocks.

- **Stocks:** Stock represents an ownership interest in a company. When you buy a stock, you want the stock to appreciate in value so that you can sell it to someone else at a higher price. Some companies pay their stockholders dividends, which are generally voluntary, not mandatory, payments.

> { "Retirement wealth is within everyone's reach." }

A Matter of Time

Retirement wealth is within everyone's reach. Just remember the following words of wisdom:

- Investing small amounts of money regularly, even $100 a month, makes a difference over time.

- Over a working career, investing $5,000 each and every year in a Roth IRA is a powerful way to make millions of dollars without the downward pressure of taxes. If you don't qualify for a Roth, you can take advantage of a loophole that permits anyone to convert to a Roth. (See the definition for "Roth IRA loophole" on page 15.) Plus, you have the option of investing in a Roth 401(k) if your company provides one.

- Fully maximizing your 401(k) plan at work is the optimal way to invest for the future, as long as you don't panic and stop investing in bad markets.

This advice is based on compounding. If you study all historical periods in the market since the Great Depression (1929–32), you'll see that long-term results are very positive. It's a matter of time.

In fact, you can take advantage of bad markets by investing small amounts of money as markets decline. When they right themselves, your returns will benefit.

But don't just take my word for it. Convince yourself.

Here are the facts:

You cannot ignore the worst market meltdown in recent memory: From October 9, 2007, through March 9, 2009, the S&P 500 Index fell 57 percent from peak to trough, the worst market period since the Great Depression. If you stuck it out until you couldn't take the bad news any longer and sold out at the bottom, you would have lost 57 percent. Many did.

If you invested monthly in a mutual fund mimicking the S&P 500 Index, beginning October 1, 2007, and selling out March 31, 2009, you would have lost more than 57 percent.

But what if you didn't sell, and, in fact, you kept buying? If you kept up your monthly investing a little longer — say, through the end of 2010 — you would have achieved an average annual return of 10.5 percent.

If you continued to invest monthly through September 30, 2013, your average annual return would have been 12.8 percent.

You don't need to know much about the markets to have achieved these returns. Any 401(k) participant could have done the same through regular payroll contributions — or more, if the plan provided a match.

YOUR INVESTMENT PROFILE

You can look at the financial markets through three prisms: the pessimist's, the optimist's, and the realist's.

A *pessimist* will see danger lurking at all times — negative events and news headlines will keep her on the sidelines. And there are always plenty of examples of bad news, such as dysfunction in Washington, economic uncertainty, accidents, wars, geopolitical unrest, and, of course, fear of the future. The pessimist stopped investing in her 401(k) at the bottom of the financial crisis and didn't get back in. Her money is still in a bank account or a CD.

An *optimist* sees only opportunity with no concern for risk. This is the type of investor who buys a "story" about a stock. During the Internet bubble, the optimist bought brand-spanking-new Internet stocks before they made profits or even sales. During the housing bubble, optimists bought real estate as it was rising *because* it was rising. In all bubbles, the optimist believes that this time, things are different — prices only go up.

A *realist* sees both sides of the coin. She is a healthy skeptic who sets reasonable goals and is happy with achieving average results over a long period of time, with the knowledge that investing is not a short-term enterprise. The realist is not persuaded by promises of quick profits. She is neither elated when markets go up nor distraught when they turn down. She ignores the news and invests based on her plan rather than someone else's. She assesses the potential risk of every investment before she puts her money to work. She watches her investments and makes decisions to sell or buy more, based on whether the investment is achieving the results she expects.

ONE WOMAN'S VIEW
JEN'S STORY: "I could rise to the task"

Jen has always depended on her husband for financial support. But then he became ill and could no longer fill that role. She reached out to me because she knew that ever since I started my column 15 years ago, I've made a practice of devoting two hours a week pro bono to respond to reader questions.

I always thought that my husband was the rock, the foundation of my life, until he became seriously ill two years ago. I knew nothing about our finances. I completely depended on him. To my amazement, I discovered with money manager Julie Jason's help and guidance that I could rise to the task. The journey was hard to embark on, but once I started, I quickly became the owner of my family's financial well-being. Julie started me with the very simple task of getting all of our account statements into a binder, and we went from there. I learned that the knowledge I needed wasn't the knowledge of external things. It was the knowledge of my family's finances. It was all about me and my husband and my family's needs and goals. Finances flowed from that examination. And they flowed easily once I got started. As I learned about our situation, I grew more and more confident in defining questions that needed to be answered and in taking steps to learn how to manage our financial future."

THE RETIREMENT-WEALTH QUIZ

1 Are you a realist, a pessimist, or an optimist when it comes to finances and investing?
  A. realist
  B. pessimist
  C. optimist

2 Are you willing to put in the time to review your personal financial situation?
  A. yes
  B. perhaps
  C. no

3 Do you believe a review can help you identify areas for potential improvement?
  A. yes
  B. perhaps
  C. no

4 Are you open to learning?
  A. yes
  B. perhaps
  C. no

5 Are you open to studying how to take advantage of compounding?
  A. yes
  B. perhaps
  C. no

6 Do you believe in your own ability to create your own financial security?
  A. yes
  B. perhaps
  C. no

You earn 5 points for every "A" answer, 3 points for every "B" answer, and 0 points for every "C" answer. If you earned 20 points or higher, you are on the road to financial security. If you earned between 12–15 points, you could do better. If you earned fewer than 8 points, you may miss out on the benefits of the time value of money.

SYSTEMATIC INVESTING

Behavioral economists tell us that inertia stops people from taking actions that can help them succeed as investors. You, however, are already on the path to securing your future: you took the first step by spending some time with me here, becoming familiar with concepts that will help you take positive actions. The most difficult part is now behind you.

No matter where you are in terms of knowledge and experience, take the time now to commit to a systematic program of investing for your future. See the "Three-Stage 30-Day Program" on the next page.

The Three-Stage 30-Day Program

Stage 1: For the next ten days, commit to organizing your papers and learning about your own financial situation. Look for areas of improvement. For example, is your company providing a 401(k) plan, but you're not taking advantage of it? Make a list of questions that you'll want to answer. Another example: ask yourself how much you are spending each month on basic needs vs. wants.

Stage 2: After completing Stage 1, take ten days to do some research on the questions you have identified when you reviewed your financial situation. For example, talk to your 401(k) provider about how to maximize your company match. Figure out how much you are spending monthly. If you were to retire this coming Monday, figure out how long you could live on your savings before needing to go back to work.

Stage 3: Now, take ten days to focus on investments. Browse the Vanguard Web site (vanguard.com) for information on investing. Research investment vehicles that track the stock market, such as Vanguard's S&P 500 Index Fund. Vanguard pioneered index funds, making them available for individual investors in 1976. For educational resources, browse Morningstar.com, Valueline.com, and the American Association of Individual Investors Web site at aaii.com.

• RESOURCES •

I've written two popular books that will help you continue your journey towards financial literacy and success. Both books have been recognized with awards for excellence in financial-literacy education. Here is a little information about each one:

- *The AARP Retirement Survival Guide: How to Make Smart Financial Decisions in Good Times and Bad* will help you start thinking about retirement finances. It is full of tools, checklists, and questions to ask that will prepare you before you make an investment. Be sure to read Chapter 6, "Can You Improve Your Situation?" That chapter will show you how to take advantage of the benefits of compounding.

- *Managing Retirement Wealth: An Expert Guide to Personal Portfolio Management in Good Times and Bad* will help you think through the differences between investing for retirement and any other type of investing you might do. Like *The AAPR Retirement Survival Guide*, this one helps people move through the process of decision making at this important time of life. The book is full of tools and resources that you will be able to put to good use right away. In the Appendix, courtesy of the AAII (the American Association of Individual Investors), you'll have information that will enable you to research individual stocks.

If you have a financial question that you'd like me to answer in my syndicated column (King Features), please e-mail me at: readers@juliejason.com.

Retirement Plan Ahead **Action Steps**

1 Put Together a Financial Binder

This handy resource should contain copies of your most recent account statements for all of your bank and brokerage accounts, as well as your retirement plans at work. If you decide to keep this information in an electronic file on your computer, be sure to password protect the document.

2 Create a Log

On your computer, create a document that contains a list of each account. Make a column for each of the following:

- Owner of the account (you alone, your spouse alone, you and your spouse jointly, in trust for you or someone else, or one(s) that will transfer on death to someone else, etc.)
- The dollar amount
- The tax nature of the account:
  - ▶ tax deferred, like a traditional IRA, 401(k), or 403(b)
  - ▶ tax exempt, like a Roth IRA or Roth 401(k)
  - ▶ taxable (neither tax deferred nor tax exempt), like an individual or joint account
- The beneficiary of the account, if there is one.

3 Review the Log

Go over all of your accounts with your spouse, if you are married, or a trusted friend or family member, if you are not. See if any organizational issues come out of the review. For example, you may notice that all of your accounts are tax deferred. That's great if you are building your retirement assets, but it also means that you will need to start saving in a taxable account as well.

4 Go Online

Check out Vanguard.com to research investment basics and study some of their offerings. Also spend time on Morningstar.com and Valueline.com, where you will find research for individual investors.

5 Join the AAII, the American Association of Individual Investors

For a modest annual fee, you will have access to exceptional investment educational materials (aaii.com).

6 Step Back to Take a Big-Picture View

Is there room for improvement? Remember: your goal is to create wealth. What can you do today to move closer to that goal?

NO PIE IN THE SKY
BY M. CINDY HOUNSELL

A top advocate for helping women save for retirement reveals the secrets to smart planning.

Lawyer M. Cindy Hounsell originally started out as a stewardess, and when her pension was frozen by Pan American World Airlines, she was amazed that other women besides her knew so little about money and retirement. So in 1996, she launched the Women's Institute for a Secure Retirement (WISER), a nonprofit that teaches women about the importance of retirement planning and how to get it done. Her work has been widely recognized. She was named one of 40 "Money Heroes" by *Money Magazine* in 2012, and *ForbesWoman* named the nonprofit Web site wiserwomen.org as one of the "Top 100 Web Sites for Women 2012." Cindy lives in Washington, DC, where her feet are firmly on the ground.

HOW TO HAVE A SMOOTH FINANCIAL LANDING
The 5 Tips You Need to Know

I started my career as a stewardess for Pan American World Airlines. It was a highly sought-after position back then, when most other career opportunities for women still involved marriage or becoming a nurse, teacher, or secretary. I traveled the world, met my share of celebrities, and reveled in the good old days when being a flight attendant was mostly glamorous and had many benefits.

I left that job after Pan Am slashed my future pension. I had always been interested in getting a law degree, and now I had a new interest in retirement issues. Realizing women were not paying attention to the effects of longevity, I saw the importance of educating women about what they needed to know and do in order to become more secure.

> "Most polls show that women who are asked about their top concern respond that it's running out of money in retirement."

So, pay attention. Especially those of you who think that finding a financial solution for a 20–30-year time frame will just take care of itself. There's a reason why most polls show that women who are asked about their top concern respond that it's running out of money in retirement. Younger women need to know what the poverty statistics are for older women and then get cracking to ensure they avoid this outcome!

PERCENTAGE OF OLDER WOMEN WITH INSUFFICIENT INCOME IN RETIREMENT:	
RACE	PERCENTAGE
White women	49%
Asian women	61%
African American women	74%
Hispanic women	75%[1]

[1] Wider Opportunities for Women. *Doing Without: Economic Insecurity and Older Americans*. No. 2: Gender. March 2012. wowonline.org/documents/ OlderAmericansGenderbriefFINAL.pdf

Try these **5 tips** to help you make a smooth financial landing in your retirement years.

Tip #1: Figure out how much income you'll need

This is one of the most important pieces of the retirement puzzle, but few people ever take the time to figure out how much they'll actually need to live on in retirement. It's really not hard, especially with all the free tools available online.

But if you don't understand what all those big numbers mean, then figure it out for yourself. For a quick, back-of-the-envelope approach, look at your current income after taxes and multiply by 20 or 30.

Example: Here's a quick approach to calculating how much income you'll need at today's spending level.

$30,000	(your income today, after taxes & other deductions)
X	20	(estimated years in retirement)
$600,000	(how much you need in retirement income)

I *don't* recommend this as a planning device, but at least it'll give you a quick view of what you'll need. Of course, the back-of-the-envelope approach doesn't deal with inflation or unexpected health costs. But it's a quick way to back into the bigger numbers.

If you want to use one of the free online calculators, check out the one on the Money pages of AARP's Web site. Go to aarp.org/work and scroll down to the AARP Retirement Calculator. It will back you into your retirement goal, based on several pieces of information, including:

- your age
- your income

- when you plan to retire
- how much you've saved
- if you expect money from a pension or other source
- your Social Security benefits (you can let the tool estimate this)

An interactive graph will show you how much you'll need and if you're on track to meet that goal. You can change the information to see how your outlook changes. Increasing your savings rate, working longer, getting a part-time job, or changing your lifestyle to a more moderate spending level can improve your retirement outlook.

> **Take Action!**
> Find out how much income you'll need in retirement. Go to aarp.org/work and click on the AARP Retirement Calculator. Or use 360 Degrees of Financial Literacy at 360financialliteracy.org.

Tip #2: Protect yourself and your future

Many of us ignore some of the best ways to build a sound financial base: through benefits provided by our employers. These can include not only health and retirement benefits, but also disability, life insurance, and flexible-spending accounts.

Many employers provide a basic level of life insurance but will allow an opportunity to purchase a higher level of coverage at an affordable price. Ask your benefits office to assess your level of coverage for both life insurance and disability — you may want it increased. Also, ask if you can keep your coverage if you leave the company.

If you are married, ask your spouse to check benefits and eligibility, too.

> **Take Action!**
> Make sure you know what your employer provides and take advantage of opportunities to help protect your future. Check out your spouse's eligibility, too. And change your benefits and your beneficiaries as changes occur in your life.

Tip #3: Save as much as you can in company-sponsored savings plans

Many employers offer retirement savings plans like 401(k)s. They can go by other names, depending where you work — the 403(b), 457, and Thrift Savings Plans provide pretty much the same opportunity to save as a 401(k).

You may get automatically enrolled in the plan, but it's more likely you'll need to sign up. Here's what to know:

- Sign up and contribute as much as you can straight from your paycheck. As a loose guide, aim to build up your savings by contributing anywhere from 10 percent to 15 percent of your income. You may not be able to save that much right away, but make it a long-term goal.

- Does your employer offer a match? For example, your company might match your contribution dollar for dollar, up to 3 percent of pay. Include this amount in your contribution planning. If you want to save 15 percent and have a 3 percent match, then aim for 12 percent of pay as your contribution.

- Invest wisely. Your plan may offer lots of investment funds. How do you choose what's right for you? Consider a "target date fund," if that's an option. This kind of fund offers an investment mix aimed at certain retirement dates, like a 2020 or a 2030 fund. But check how that mix is divided between stocks and bonds.

- If you leave your job, roll your account into your new employer's plan, or into an IRA. Don't cash it out — even if the amount seems small.

Take Action!
Make good use of your retirement savings plan at work. Contribute as much as you can, invest wisely, and try never to use that money to bankroll today's needs. If you leave your employer, roll your account into a new plan or into an IRA (individual retirement account).

Tip #4: Understand how to get the most from your Social Security benefit

Social Security is the first line of defense against poverty in retirement. Millions of women count on it as their only source of income in their older years. But it was never meant to be the sole source of a retiree's income. Social Security retirement benefits replace about 40 percent of a worker's income, on average.

You may be eligible to receive Social Security retirement benefits in several ways. To earn the right to them, you or your spouse must have worked at least ten years (or "40 quarters," in Social Security lingo).

Here is a rundown of ways you may be able to claim Social Security:

Retirement benefits
- Benefit is based on your own work record, unless 50 percent

of your spouse's benefit is higher; you receive the higher amount

- Earliest claiming age is 62, but benefits are reduced permanently

- "Full retirement age" is between 65 and 67, depending on your birth year

- Delay benefits to age 70 to maximize the monthly benefit amount

---

Age Matters!

Jean's Social Security full retirement age is 66. Here's how her benefit amount changes, based on when she retires:

Age 62 (early retirement):	$ 758
Age 66 (full retirement age):	$1,000
Age 70 (latest):	$1,320

Benefits if your spouse or ex-spouse dies

If you are widowed, you may be eligible for survivor benefits. These benefits are equal to 100 percent of your spouse's (or former spouse's) retirement benefit. Here are your claiming options:

- Benefits begin immediately upon your spouse's death if you are raising either a disabled child, or any children under age 16 (note: this benefit is available even if your spouse worked less than ten years)

- Benefits begin at age 50 if you are disabled

- Benefits begin at your full retirement age if you are unmarried (note: if you remarry after age 60, this will not affect your survivor benefits)

- Reduced benefits are available at age 60

Benefits if you are divorced

If your marriage lasted at least ten years, you may be eligible for Social Security retirement benefits based on your ex-husband's work record:

- You can receive spousal benefits on his work record if you remain unmarried, regardless of his marital status
- If your ex-husband is deceased and you are unmarried, you can collect survivor benefits, which is 100 percent of his retirement benefit (vs. 50 percent if you collect spousal benefits while he is alive)

> **Take Action!**
> Find out your "full retirement age" for Social Security benefits. Consider the impact of your retirement age on your Social Security benefit. You can get an estimate of your benefit from ssa.gov/estimator.

Tip #5: Take advantage of the Saver's Tax Credit

You might be eligible for a federal tax credit for your retirement contributions. It's called the Saver's Tax Credit, and it's geared to middle- and lower-income taxpayers. It could be worth up to $1,000 for you.

So, what's a tax credit? It cuts down the taxes you owe dollar for dollar. If you owe $500 in taxes, a $500 tax credit would mean you owe nothing. If you don't owe taxes when you complete your tax return, then it won't be of value to you. This means the tax credit is "nonrefundable."

To claim this credit, you must be at least 18 and not a full-time student. You cannot be claimed as a dependent on someone else's tax return. And you must have contributed to a qualified retirement plan (like a 401(k) or 403(b) plan) or IRA last year.

As with most tax credits, the Saver's Tax Credit is not just a straightforward amount. Its value to you depends on your income and your filing status. The credit amount ranges from 10 percent to 50 percent of your eligible savings contribution (for amounts up to $2,000).

Most women are unaware of the Saver's Tax Credit. One survey found that 88 percent of women have never heard of it.[2] If you're one of them, you could be missing out on an opportunity to cut your tax bill. To learn more, visit irs.gov and look for Form 8880.

ADJUSTED GROSS INCOME LIMITS FOR SAVER'S TAX CREDIT TAX YEAR 2013[3]			
	JOINT FILERS	HEAD OF HOUSEHOLD	SINGLE OR MARRIED FILING SEPARATELY
50% OF CONTRIBUTION	$0–$35,500	$0–$26,625	$0–$17,750
20% OF CONTRIBUTION	$35,501–$38,500	$26,626–$28,875	$17,751–$19,250
10% OF CONTRIBUTION	$38,501–$59,000	$28,876–$44,250	$19,251–$29,500
NO CREDIT	$59,001 AND OVER	$44,251 AND OVER	$29,501 AND OVER

If you're eligible for the Saver's Tax Credit based on your income, contribute to your work-based savings plan or an IRA to claim it when you file your next tax return. Use Form 8880 a tirs.gov.

[2] Transamerica Center for Retirement Studies. *Women: Let's Talk About Retirement. The 12th Annual Transamerica Retirement Survey.* January 2, 2012.

[3] IRS. Retirement Topics — Retirement Savings Contributions Credit (Saver's Tax Credit). http://www.irs.gov/Retirement-Plans/Plan-Participant,-Employee/Retirement-Topics-Retirement-Savings-Contributions-Credit-%28Saver%E2%80%99s-Credit%29

Retirement Plan Ahead **Action Steps**

1 Figure Out How Much Income You'll Need

For a quick, back-of-the-envelope approach, look at your current income after taxes and multiply by 20 or 30 years. For a more comprehensive approach, go to aarp.org/work and click on the AARP Retirement Calculator. Or use a calculator created by 360 Degrees of Financial Literacy at 360financialliteracy.org.

2 Protect Yourself and Your Future

Ask your benefits office at work to assess your level of coverage for both life insurance and disability. Also, ask if you can keep your coverage if you leave the company. If you are married, ask your spouse to check benefits and eligibility, too.

3 Save as Much as You Can in Company-Sponsored Savings Plans

Participate in your retirement savings plan at work. Contribute as much as you can, invest wisely, and roll it into a new plan or an IRA if you leave your employer.

4 Understand How to Get the Most from Your Social Security Benefit

Find out your full retirement age for Social Security benefits. Consider the impact of your retirement age on your benefit. Get an estimate of your benefit from ssa.gov/ estimator.

5 Take Advantage of the Saver's Tax Credit

If you're eligible for the Saver's Tax Credit based on your income, contribute to your work-based savings plan or an IRA to claim it when you file your next tax return.

A big reason I became an advocate for women's retirement security is because of the genuine lack of understanding among millions of women about funding retirement. Ladies, remember this: hope is *not* a financial plan. There is no pie in the sky, so keep your feet firmly planted on the ground and take action today!

THINKING AHEAD . . . WHAT'S NEXT?

BY DORIAN MINTZER, M.S.W., Ph.D., BCC

This leading retirement expert reveals how to begin preparing for a meaningful retirement – and the many rewarding options available to you.

Dr. Dorian Mintzer is an experienced therapist; retirement-transition, relationship, and executive coach; consultant; writer; and speaker. Her expertise in adult development, life planning, positive psychology, and creativity, combined with her life experiences, have led to her passion for helping individuals and couples navigate the "second half of life." She is the founder of two virtual communities and the coauthor of *The Couple's Retirement Puzzle*. Her Web site is revolutionizeretirement.com.

LOOKING AT THE FUTURE
Welcome to Retirement Planning 101

For women reading this book who are in their 40s or 50s, congratulations for taking action now about your retirement. Many of you have choices that your mothers didn't have. Your generation is living longer, with women still outliving men, and there are many more dual-career relationships. Women often enter the labor force later and feel "in their prime" in their 40s, 50s, and 60s, not necessarily wanting to retire at the "traditional retirement age" of 62 or 65, since they like their work and/or know they need to continue to work so they don't outlive their money. Others want to work in different ways, perhaps using their skills for "encore careers" or volunteer work.

In addition, many women no longer want to live their husband's retirement dream — they want their own dream. We're also seeing more divorces in the over-50 population, partly because some women are no longer dependent financially on their partner and don't want to stay in an unhappy marriage for another 30 or more years.

Although the boomer generation is considered "the best and the brightest," a large proportion aren't financially able to retire. Many are caught in the "sandwich generation," helping their children as well as their parents, and they haven't realistically saved for their own retirement years. One of the secrets I've learned in my own clinical work with women in their middle years, combined with the experiences of the "leading edge boomers" (born between 1946 and 1955), is that it's never too early to start planning ahead. The more that you can think intentionally about retirement, the greater the likelihood that you'll have better life choices.

REDEFINING "RETIREMENT"

The concept of retirement has already changed in the 21st century and may continue to change over the next 20 years. The term "retirement" may soon become obsolete — but it's currently the term people use. In many ways it's now less important what

{ "'Retirement' is no longer a destination, but more of a journey." }

you're retiring *from* and more important to consider what you're retiring *to*. Retirement is not "retiring from life," but perhaps retiring from work (or the way that you were working). "Retirement" is no longer a destination, but more of a journey.

Whether your role has been primarily as a mother and/or in the workforce, there's a normal internal shift that begins to occur as we age that may alter your interests, values, and priorities. Some people liken it to the changes of adolescence, although, with our added years, we have the wisdom, experiences, and perspective that adolescents lack. We may find ourselves asking the same questions they do, such as *Who am I? What's my identity? Who are my friends? What's important to me? What do I want to do? Where do I want to live?*

Also, nowadays, many are deciding not to marry, or they choose to have children alone, while others favor alternative lifestyles and commitments. There is no "one way." What is similar, however, is that we all need a social life and community, whether we're alone or in a relationship. As Hillary Rodham Clinton has said, "It takes a village" — not just to raise children, but throughout our lives.

In his book Flourish, Martin E. P. Seligman writes that well-being is a combination of connection, engagement and purpose, and meaning. Work and/or active parenting may have provided that combination (along with stress at times, too!). Once that "work" is less important, how will you maintain your sense of well-being?

If you're in your 40s or 50s, it's easy to think that your retirement is a long way off in the future and that you don't have to start thinking about it now. But, as I've said earlier, the secret to successful retirement planning is getting a running start — the sooner you start preparing, the better your later years will be.

Getting to Know Yourself

One of first steps in your planning for retirement is to take time to get to know yourself and what you want for your future. Begin by asking some of these questions:

- ▶ "Who will I be" once my active parenting and/or my role at work changes?

- ▶ Who will I socialize with, if I no longer actively focus on my family or my work?

- ▶ How will I structure my life so I feel connected, engaged, and with a sense of purpose and meaning in life?

- ▶ What are my values, interests, and goals?

- ▶ What's *really* important to me? What have I always wanted to do?

- ▶ What has held me back?

- ▶ What kind of relationships do I want with family and friends?

- ▶ How do I want to give back in meaningful ways to my community?

- ▶ How do I want to be remembered – in big or small ways?

Once you've answered the questions above, you're ready for the next step in your "prep process" — doing a "life review."

A life review is a way of taking stock of your life at this moment in time. If we honestly know where we've come from, we can start to discover where we're going. This kind of inventory is every bit as important as doing a review of your finances — you're assessing your "emotional portfolio."

Your Life Review

....

▶ What are three things you're most proud of in your life?

▶ How have you handled transitions in your past? Do you have more difficulty with the endings, the unknowns, or the new beginnings?

▶ Name three to five of the most important people in your life. What makes them important to you?

▶ Do you allow yourself to feel gratitude and forgiveness, or do you tend to hold on to grudges?

▶ What has given pleasure and purpose and meaning to your life?

▶ How have you built connection and community into your life?

CREATE MEANINGFUL CONNECTIONS
Caring Communities

Meaningful connections can help make a retirement more fulfilling. Research shows that isolation in retirement is a common problem — for women as well as men. A large number of women in the boomer generation don't have children and/or family members nearby. Even if you do, you can't necessarily count on them for support. In addition, many of us want to be independent for as long as possible and don't want to ask for help. However, life changes, and we may need help for ourselves and/or a family member. You may be fortunate enough to rely on relatives, but it's also important to create an "extended family" of friends for support and social life.

There are Web-based and community-based models for "caring communities." For example, The Transition Network (thetransitionnetwork.org) has developed a program called "The Caring Collaborative," which has become a model around the country. People help others, knowing that they can also count on being helped when the need arises. This is particularly helpful for women living alone. A great example of a Web-based caring community is lotsahelpinghands.com, which was developed by a husband when his wife had breast cancer and friends said they wanted to help. I can vouch for it; I used it to help coordinate care when a friend was sick. In addition, many faith-based organizations have "caring communities" that you can participate in and also call upon when you need help. We all need to feel needed and to have something that gets us out of bed in the morning.

> "We all need to feel needed and to have something that gets us out of bed in the morning."

Many of us, growing up during the 1960s and '70s and influenced by the women's movement, recognize the importance of women friends and connectedness. It's special to have "old friends from the past" as well as new friends as we age. Not all relationships work, so we need to figure out when to "let go" of relationships that aren't good for us. Social media has also created a way for people to stay connected and find each other from the past. I recall how amazing it was for an old friend from 55 years ago to find me through Facebook! New friends can be developed through activities you choose, whether it be working, volunteering, spending time at the museum, going to films, joining or starting a book group, etc. Our need for social connection can be realized in our choice about where to live as well as in the way we approach the world through our activities. There are endless possibilities for connection.

> "Who can you count on
> for support when you
> experience the
> 'curveballs in life'?"

There are so many options for living that weren't even around when our mothers were turning 65. For example, senior and multigenerational *cohousing communities* are beginning to spring up across the United States, giving retirees who don't want to feel alone in their later years the opportunity to have their own home and to also share a separate building with common areas (such as a kitchen, living room, activity room, and even a room for a community caregiver). This and many other exciting options — such as *the village model, intentional community*, and *shared housing* — are important steps in helping to prevent isolation by building community in retirement. You can read more about the housing options available to you in the essays by Sally Abrahms (page 48) and Kathryn McCamant (page 56).

In addition to considering different housing options for the future, think about other ways to build new connections or deepen long-standing relationships. You are doing something good for yourself when you reach out to others.

THE "MAKING CONNECTIONS" CHECKLIST

The following activities will help you to develop and strengthen relationships:

- ☐ *Learn a new skill, so you exercise your body, brain, and spirit (dancing, art, music, writing, or a new language)*
- ☐ *Sign up for classes through a lifelong-learning program in your community*
- ☐ *Form a book group or join one that exists*

- [ ] *Develop a "buddy system" with a friend to exercise or join a gym*
- [ ] *Go to programs at your local museum*
- [ ] *Volunteer*
- [ ] *Go to fund-raisers that support causes important to you*
- [ ] *Participate in your faith-based organization or a spiritual community*
- [ ] *Take trips that involve an activity you enjoy, learning opportunities, and/or service projects*

ONE WOMAN'S VIEW
JUDY'S STORY: Finding "a whole new calling"

Judy, age 52, a married mother of two children — one a junior in high school and another in college — was feeling anxious as she anticipated the end to her "active parenting" and began to give serious thought to her retirement years. She loved her roles as a mother and a lawyer, but realized she no longer felt as passionate about law and wasn't sure how much longer she wanted to stay in that career. She asked herself, "Who will I be when both children are gone and I retire from my profession?" She saw that a number of her retired friends were happy in their new freedom, and others seemed to be unhappy and overwhelmed. She had done some volunteer work over the years, but felt that she wanted and needed to earn an income during her retirement years to help with family expenses.

Judy broached this subject with her husband. She told him her heart was not in her law practice and that she wanted to start to think about retiring from law once both children were no longer living at home. In order to help Judy think about what she might do in the future, he encouraged her to take time to consider the interests she had in the past. "What would you have done if you didn't go to law school?" he asked. She realized that she always loved going to films, and that she particularly loved documentaries. She decided that she didn't have to be retired before doing something else. As she continued practicing law, she decided to take adult-ed courses at night to learn about film production. She then volunteered at a local TV station in her town. To enhance her skills, she enrolled in a film program at a college that was close by. Eventually, her volunteer work at the TV station led to an offer for a part-time job there. Judy left her practice to take the job and to pursue her newly developing passion. She had found a whole new calling in her life that would give excitement to her retirement years.

Retirement **Plan Ahead** Action Steps

1 Take Stock of Your "Emotional Portfoilo"

Begin to think about the next phase of your life by doing a "life review." Clarify what's important to you in the various areas of your life, so you're able to live your life with intention and purpose.

2 Find a Financial Planner

Get your finances and legal documents in order. If you feel you need help in becoming more financially literate, check out adult-ed classes in your area. Or perhaps your book group can discuss a book on saving and investing strategies for retirement. Also, don't be ashamed if you don't know how to balance your checkbook — ask a friend to help you.

3 Discuss Your Important Issues

Have crucial conversations with those important to you (for example, your partner, adult children, siblings, friends, or professionals) about retirement issues, such as where to live, health concerns, and financial challenges.

4 Explore Housing Options

Research the various housing options to figure out what might be good for you. For example, go online to check out the Cohousing Association of the United States (cohousing.org), intentional communities (agingincommunity.org), the village network concept (vtvnetwork.org, which helps you stay in your own home), and continuing-care retirement communities (retirement.org).

5 Learn About Caring Communities

Find out more about "caring communities" by visiting the Web sites for thetransitionnetwork.org and lotsahelpinghands.com.

I encourage you to embrace this next stage of life with openness to possibilities. Even though we have the gift of these "bonus years," don't waste them. Take charge of yourself, whether alone or partnered, and create a fulfilling "second half of life."

GIVE ME SHELTER — AND MORE!

BY SALLY ABRAHMS

An award-winning writer on boomers and longtime contributor to AARP looks at exciting housing options for retirees.

Sally Abrahms writes on boomer and senior housing, caregiving, and 50+ work for consumer and corporate clients. Her pieces have appeared in *TIME*, *Newsweek*, the *New York Times*, the *Wall Street Journal*, and *USA Today*, and on Forbes.com and *Huffington Post*. Sally blogs weekly for AARP and biweekly for Intel-GE's Care Innovations. She is the author of two books. Check out her Web site at sallyabrahms.com.

PLAN B

My adult children live in California, Florida, and New York. My husband and I are in the town nearest Boston. We love it here; they love it there.

If I could shrink our five-bedroom Colonial, put a bedroom and bath on the first floor, and get the kids to move back, I would live happily ever after. But to paraphrase the Rolling Stones, you might not always get what you want. That leaves Plan B.

Like many of you, I'm not sure what that is. But if I'm thinking about moving in the future, I need to know what my options are. And so do you.

{ "I need to know what
my options are." }

For Mom and Dad's generation, living alone and being independent in later life is a source of pride. But baby boomers are different. They have called the shots at every stage of their lives and have no intention of taking aging lying down!

HOUSING OPTIONS

For those in their 40s, 50s, and 60s, retirement and the decades ahead are about community and growing old together. Most of us don't want to depend on — okay, burden — our kids the way some feel our parents have (unintentionally) done with us. What's more, we may not be dying to uproot ourselves from the people or place where we have meaningful connections.

{ "[Mulitgenerational housing
is] a way to avoid isolation in
old age, and pooling money
goes farther." }

Fortunately, there are plenty of housing choices and there will be more down the road. Experts predict there will be all sorts of communities where people with the same values or interests will live. That could be dog lovers, Jimmy Buffett fans, gourmands, political or environmental activists, or cruise-ship enthusiasts. (There's already a place for nudists in Florida that is fleshing out an assisted-living project!)

Here's why there will be more housing models:

- Statistics show that 90 percent of people want to age in place (in their community or their home).
- The pool of family caregivers is shrinking, while one-third of the boomer population will be single as they face old age (widowed, divorced, never married).
- Since 1990, the divorce rate for those 50+ has doubled.
- Fewer women are having children; if they do, the adult kids may live thousands of miles away.
- The average private room in a nursing home costs $94,170 a year, a semiprivate room is $82,855 a year, and assisted living is $41,124 a year, with health-care costs soaring.

Today, those facing "retirement" plan to stay active, develop or maintain relationships and interests, keep learning, and have fun as long as they can. Increasingly, boomers are moving to nearby suburban town centers or cities where they have access to public transportation and can walk to shops, restaurants, movies, and for some, their office. (They're steering away from being car dependent.)

Arizona and Florida aren't looking so hot any more. Being near the action or family (grandkids) or friends is looking hotter.

I've written on boomer and senior housing for years. These are the coolest housing models out there:

Cohousing

How it works: A group of people buy land together and help design their community. There are 20 or so private homes clustered together with welcoming front porches that face one another, to foster community as well as informal, daily interaction. Members make rules and decisions by consensus, and manage and maintain the property. Cohousing communities are either multigenerational (more than 100 nationwide) or age 50+ (less than ten).

Residents own (or sometimes rent) their homes or condos and jointly own some outdoor space and a "common house." This central building has a kitchen and a dining room, where members can eat together a couple of times a week, as well as a living room and whatever else the community chooses. That might be a music or art studio; a workout, media, or sewing room; or a guest room or two.

The appeal: There's as much privacy (you have your own place) or group time as you want. Shared common space and resources are both good for the planet and your pocketbook.

• RESOURCES •

- The Cohousing Association of the United States cohousing.org, (812) 618-2646

- The Cohousing Company, cohousingco.com, (530) 265-9980

- *Creating Cohousing* by Kathryn McCamant (see her essay in this book on page 56) and Charles Durrett

Multigenerational Housing

How it works: At least two adult generations or a grandparent and at least one other generation live under the same roof. Some builders offer two master suites and a den or family room that can morph into a bedroom on the first floor.

The appeal: This arrangement can bring the generations closer. There's peace of mind knowing you or your parents are well taken care of and don't need institutional care. There could be built-in child care and eldercare. Though for some families this option could result in a bit too much togetherness, it's definitely a way to avoid isolation in old age, and pooling money goes further.

• RESOURCES •

- Home builder Lennar's "Next Gen" model is two houses in one, to promote multigenerational housing. lennarnextgen.com

Shared Housing

How it works: It's like dorm life for grown-ups. Women, who may be friends or strangers, move in together to save money and have companionship. Often, there are more than two people who share, and it may be someone's house or a place that's new to all. It's usually a rental arrangement, but could be group ownership. Finances, food, meals, overnight guests, cleanliness, pets, and noise are all issues that must be negotiated. Increasingly, older men and women are also moving in together in nonromantic relationships; it's sometimes a married (or not) couple with others who are single (referred to as "cohouseholding").

The appeal: You can live in a neighborhood or house you wouldn't otherwise be able to afford. You also split chores, have someone to feed your cat if you're away, and have people who get to know and care about you.

• RESOURCES •

- Women for Living in Community Network, Marianne Kilkenny, womenlivingincommunity.com

- Sharing Housing, www.sharinghousing.com
- *Sharing Housing: A Guidebook for Finding and Keeping Good Housemates* by Annamarie Pluhar
- The CoHouseholding Project ozragland.com/shared-households.html
- *My House, Our House: Living Far Better for Far Less in a Cooperative Household* by Louise S. Machinist, Jean McQuillin, and Karen M. Bush

University-Based Retirement Communities

How it works: If you always wanted to go to Stanford, Cornell, or Dartmouth, keep them in mind as options when you retire. There are more than 60 UBRCs on or near college campuses that offer a continuum of care, from independent to assisted living to skilled nursing. Most residents are in their 70s and 80s+; some, but certainly not all, are retired professors or alumni. They share a love of learning and can take classes with 20-somethings at the college and have lectures at their facility. They're welcome at sporting and cultural events on campus and get the rich benefits of an intergenerational environment.

The appeal: You're living in a college town with activities galore. With three levels of care, you never have to move.

• RESOURCES •

- The Kendal Corporation www.kendal.org/living/communitiesincollegetowns.aspx (610) 335-1200

The Village Movement

How it works: In the Village Movement, you get to stay in your own home or apartment and have support and ample social opportunities. To join these grassroots organizations, you pay an average of $500 per year for a single membership, or $650 for a household. Call one number to get whatever you need: for example, referrals for house cleaners, dog walkers, drivers, neighborhood yoga classes, or specialists to make your house more age friendly. There may be group lunches, evening events, trips to museums or the theater, or long-distance travel. There are around 110 separate Villages nationwide that are part of the Village-to-Village Network. This organization provides peer-to-peer support and helps communities establish their own villages. There are additional village-type groups that are small and more informal.

The appeal: All service providers are vetted and usually provide a discount to Village members — this perk is attracting boomers. It's the best of both worlds: a way to age in place yet not feel isolated.

• RESOURCES •

- Village-to-Village Network, vtvnetwork.org (617) 299-9NET

{ "[The Village Movement is] the best of both worlds: a way to age in place yet not feel isolated." }

Retirement   Plan Ahead   **Action Steps**

1 Decide If You Want to Stay in Your House

If not, where do you see yourself living as you get closer to your retirement years? Do you know where you might want to be?

2 Think About Your Ideal Situation

What do you like about where you live now? What don't you like? If you can no longer drive or don't want to, how will you get around? Is there public transportation? Are there people nearby to engage with?

3 Figure Out Your Finances

Can you afford to stay in your house if you want? If you don't have a handle on your money, sprint to a financial planner.

4 Consider Who Will Care for You If You Need Help

Do you want to live near your adult children or friends (or with them)? Do you have something else in mind?

5 Start Your Research Now, So You'll Have Resources for Later

Knowledge is power and gives you more options.

COHOUSING: CREATE YOUR OWN RETIREMENT COMMUNITY

BY KATHRYN McCAMANT

The renowned architect who helped introduce the concept of "cohousing" to the U.S. shows how it can benefit retirees.

Kathryn McCamant, a licensed architect, coauthored the seminal book *Cohousing: A Contemporary Approach to Housing Ourselves* with her husband, Charles Durrett. Together they introduced cohousing to North America in 1987, and have since consulted on over 50 cohousing communities. In 2011, they released *Creating Cohousing: Building Sustainable Communities* (New Society Press), which covers their 20 years of experience creating cohousing communities across North America. Kathryn's company, CoHousing Partners, is a real-estate consulting firm specializing in these sustainable communities. She has worked as an architect, developer, and consultant for dozens of communities, as well as lecturing and offering workshops for forming groups. Kathryn has lived in cohousing herself for over 20 years. Visit her Web site at cohousingpartners.com.

CREATING A COHOUSING COMMUNITY

We often dream of adventures and projects we'll do when we finally get to retire. But what is the place we come home to, the base that will sustain us, especially when we are working less?

Today, women are living more independent lives than ever before. We have careers, we can travel alone in much of the world, we may or may not get married, and we may or may not have children. But all this freedom can also mean we no longer have the family base that has been the traditional community we could fall back on as we age. If we have kids, they may live far away, caught up in their own busy lives. Now, we must be more deliberate about creating our own communities; finding our tribe.

> { **"Now, we must be more deliberate about creating our own communities; finding our tribe."** }

Some proactive adults are creating their own retirement communities by moving to a cohousing neighborhood. By combining the privacy of individual homes with extensive common facilities, cohousing neighborhoods become authentic communities where neighbors support each other and share day-to-day tasks, celebrations, and life's transitions. Typically ranging in size from 8 to 35 homes, these communities are small enough that you can really know everyone, and they can fit into an existing neighborhood.

Since the first cohousing communities were created in the early 1990s, more than 125 have been built across North America. Most of these are intergenerational communities with residents of all ages. As the boomer generation begins reaching its retirement years, however, we are seeing increasing interest in adult-oriented cohousing neighborhoods designed to draw on the many social and practical advantages of living in a community. One of the key aspects is that it enhances people's ability to stay in their own homes as they age. Depending on your preferences, you may choose an intergenerational community, typically with lots of children, or an adult-oriented community that focuses on the needs and lifestyle of older adults — both options have much to offer as we age.

One of the greatest benefits of cohousing neighborhoods is proximity. We have all created some community for ourselves. We are, after all, social beings. But today we tend to drive to our community, whether that is getting together with friends or family, or attending church or spiritual practices. We even drive to exercise. Not only does being dependent on driving eat up much of our day, but as we get older, our dependence on the car begins to limit our lives more and more. At first, we no longer want to drive at night. Then, a small accident like a twisted ankle makes it hard to drive for a few weeks. All of a sudden, we go from being busy, independent adults to being dependent on others driving across town to help us out with household chores. But what if you had not one, but a collection of friendly neighbors next door willing to help? You are likely not only to get their help going to the grocery store, but also the pleasure of their company over tea or an invitation to go out to the movies.

> "[Cohousing] enhances people's ability to stay in their own homes as they age."

THE COHOUSING EXPERIENCE
Nevada City Cohousing

I was first introduced to the cohousing concept over 30 years ago, as an architecture student studying for a year in Denmark. After seeing their communities, my partner, Chuck

Durrett, and I decided that this was the kind of neighborhood we wanted to live in, and we thought it addressed many of the challenges of our modern, single-family lifestyle — whether raising kids or growing older. Over the last 25 years, we have written several books and worked as architects, project managers, and developers for dozens of cohousing communities, as well as living in our own. Through this experience, a number of things stand out for me.

First, many people can imagine living in a community with friends, but they have a hard time imagining living with people they don't already know. And yet, our experience has shown it is very difficult to get a group of existing friends to move at the same time to the same place. I urge people to explore cohousing with those interested in doing it on their timeline, in the same region, whoever that may be. While your new neighbors will never replace your long-term friends, you may find they make great new friends, and that good neighbors that enrich your life don't even have to be good friends.

Second, people hold back because of their fears about commitment and loss of privacy. But those who live in cohousing don't find them to be big issues at all. At Nevada City Cohousing, an intergenerational community of 34 homes where I live, it's easy for me to shut the door and have my own time when I need that. I still have my privacy, but I have gained a wonderful, easily accessible community just outside my door.

Third, and perhaps most important, beyond the practical benefits are the deeper rewards of sharing life's journey with neighbors. We came together to share the goal of living in an authentic community: neighbors who don't run from the deeper discussions, who show up for management meetings, and who contribute every day in a multitude of small and large ways toward creating this wonderful place.

In my own community, I have noticed that we are particularly good at supporting the caregiving spouse, often an overlooked and very stressful situation when one's partner is sick over a long time period. Community dinners and other social activities reduce the feeling of isolation that can come with long-term caretaking. And being right next door makes it easy to pitch in by picking up something at the store or being "on call" so that the caregiver can take a break.

One of the things I most enjoy about living in a community is learning from my elders by watching how they deal with life's challenges. It is, after all, the rituals we share with neighbors and family to mark life's milestones that bring meaning to it all. One of the most powerful community experiences was the death of my neighbor Jean.

ONE WOMAN'S VIEW
REMEMBERING JEAN:
"She showed us how to do death graciously"

Jean was a truly "Outrageous Older Woman" and wore the T-shirt to prove it. She showed us how to do death graciously. At 80, she had a BIG birthday party in the common house. Shortly after that, it became clear that her cancer treatments weren't working. She spent the next six months preparing to pass on to whatever comes next. With the help of a roommate, Jean stayed in her cohousing home, visiting with family and friends until the end. She was an inspiration in speaking her needs clearly — when she wanted visitors, and when she didn't. I remember her asking for the young girls to come play their violins for her one afternoon. We got a little confused when she sent word out that she was no longer eating, and then got hungry and started eating again — craving spicy Chinese shrimp. Then the time came, and Jean passed on peacefully in her sleep, at home. Her daughter and a neighbor dressed her in a beautiful, very yellow sheath, and we said our goodbyes, one last time. Then, a few days later, we gathered as a community in our common house to remember Jean and share a cup of tea. Friends of all ages were there, telling stories, sharing memories. And so we learned how do to a "good" death from our neighbor Jean.

{ "We came together to share the goal of living in an authentic community." }

FOR PROACTIVE ADULTS
Wolf Creek Lodge – a cohousing community

Wolf Creek Lodge is a 30-unit adult-oriented community completed in 2012 in Grass Valley, California, in the Sierra Foothills. Residents, ranging in age from 56 to 89, participated in the design and development of the community, so most already knew each other when they moved in. They immediately organized community dinners several times a week, a morning coffee klatch, carpooling to yoga classes, and hikes. As a self-managed condominium community, these activities are not scheduled by a social director, but rather by the residents themselves when they run into each other on the walkway or over their community e-mail. By working together, Lodge residents greatly improve their ability to stay independent in their own homes.

Just a few months after moving in, one of the Lodge residents had a medical emergency. Upon her return home, she wrote: *"I was overwhelmed by the kindness and help I received. [Friends from the Lodge] took me to the hospital and spent many boring hours till I was admitted there. They are supplying me with food and go grocery shopping, fold my laundry, etc. My neighbor Mike takes out my compost and garbage every day. I can hardly breathe before there is another good deed. My granddaughter Sonja, who came to visit me just when I needed it, was so impressed with all the wonderful people who keep showing up. There is no place like Wolf Creek Lodge!"*

The Oakcreek Senior Cohousing Community

In Stillwater, Oklahoma, the Oakcreek Senior Cohousing Community developed guiding principles for their 24-home development that include "active, healthy living for body, mind, and spirit; lifelong learning and growth; interdependence, mutual support, and compassion; community service; and environmental sustainability and stewardship." The neighborhood design provides a balance between personal privacy and making it easy to know your neighbors, with large front porches and walking lanes between the homes.

> *"The house I raised my kids in is too big now that it's just me, and besides I want to live in a community where I know all my neighbors and we can live interdependently to age successfully — and have a fun and purposeful second half of life at the same time."*

— Pat Darlington, a founding member of the Oakcreek Senior Cohousing Community and a licensed psychologist with a private practice in Stillwater.

COLLABORATING ON A SUSTAINABLE LIFESTYLE

Most of these communities include in their vision the goal of living more sustainably. I have found that for those who are older, this is often a particularly strong goal as they strive to leave less resource-intensive housing models as an example for their children and grandchildren. The communities include not only energy-efficient heating and cooling systems and solar panels, but also consider the air quality of the building materials, and their ability to buy less thorough cooperation.

Through collaboration, we can do so much more than we can alone, whether that means implementing a more energy-efficient heating system that serves the whole building, driving less, or only having to buy one lawn mower.

REAPING THE BENEFITS OF COMMUNITY

Over the last several decades, numerous studies have highlighted the benefits of having a strong social network to help us deal with stress, recover from illness, and live longer. Thus, not only can a community encourage healthy eating and exercise, and keep the mind stimulated, but the social network that's inherent in cohousing living may also help us to lead a healthier, longer life. Being part of a community may very well be the most important thing you can do for yourself, whether now or as you enter your retirement years.

> "The social network that's inherent in cohousing living may also help us to lead a healthier, longer life."

In my own intergenerational community, Nevada City Cohousing, I especially enjoy watching the kids play, now that my husband and I are empty nesters. At the upcoming annual Harvest Festival, I will attempt to organize the kids to plant 350 spring bulbs, and then set up the grapevine wreath-decorating booth. By building my community relationships now, while I'm in my mid-50s, I will reap the rewards later when I may need an extra hand. I find that this is one of the keys to successfully aging in a community: plan and move in *before* you need help and while you still have the energy to build your community relationships.

COHOUSING QUESTIONNAIRE			
The Silver Sage Village in North Boulder, Colorado, posted this reflective questionaire on their Web site to help people explore whether the community would be a good fit for them.			
	AGREE	NEUTRAL	DISAGREE
I try to be as physically active as my health allows.			
I am interested in learning new things.			
I value a sense of community with others.			
I would like to participate in some group activities.			
I would like to continue my volunteer work or start a new project.			
I would like to give and receive caring support as I age.			
I value the environment and act accordingly (recycling, etc.).			
I would like to further develop my gifts and talents and encourage others to develop theirs.			
I am open to change.			
I appreciate diversity in a community.			
I would like to help create and maintain a community.			
If you agree with most of these statements, you might be a good fit for membership in the Silver Sage community.			

Retirement Plan Ahead **Action Steps**

If these ideas about cohousing interest you, how do you begin to put thought into action? I've listed a number of resources below. Use them to find out about communities in your area, or other regions that you might consider moving to in retirement. If you are moving to a new area, cohousing can provide you with local ties that would otherwise take decades to build. Read our books, and check out as many communities as you can. Visiting communities is very helpful to see what most resonates with you. Adult oriented or intergenerational? Urban or rural? How urban? And most important, how do you feel about the other people in the community? Then, when you are ready . . . jump in! You don't have to wait until retirement.

1 Read About Cohousing

Get a copy of the books: *The Senior Cohousing Handbook: A Community Approach to Independent Living* by Charles Durrett; and *Creating Cohousing: Building Sustainable Communities* by Kathryn McCamant and Charles Durrett (New Society Press).

2 Check Resources

Research available resources from The Cohousing Association of the Unites States at cohousing.org; look for workshops, conferences, tours, and events.

3 Visit Cohousing Communities

You can find a list of existing and forming groups on the Directory page at cohousing.org.

4 Organize a Workshop

To get a cohousing community started in your region, put together a preliminary meeting or workshop to see if others in your area are interested in the idea.

5 Start Your Own Cohousing Community

Contact the author, Kathryn McCamant, to find out more about how she can help you get your cohousing community off the ground. You can e-mail her at info@cohousingpartners.com.

RETIRING SOLO

BY SARA ZEFF GEBER, Ph.D., CRC

An esteemed retirement-planning coach provides valuable advice to help single women have a satisfying retirement.

Dr. Sara Zeff Geber is a life-planning and transition expert for baby boomers. She coaches individuals and couples, leads retirement-transition workshops, and speaks to groups about how to be proactive in planning for the second half of life. In her role as the founder of LifeEncore, Sara works cooperatively with financial planners and estate attorneys to provide a 360-degree perspective on how the baby-boom generation is reinventing aging. Sara is on the Board of Directors for the Life Planning Network (LPN) and is a sponsoring partner and active member in the Silicon Valley Chapter of the Financial Planning Association.

BEING SINGLE IN RETIREMENT

Are you a single woman? If you are, you are in good company! Over half of all women in the U.S. today are living solo. That translates into over 50 million women living without a husband. Part of this startling statistic is due to women marrying later, but a significant part of it is due to divorce, widowhood, and choice. Women have so many more options today than they did in previous generations, and that has led to far more women of all ages saying "no, thanks" to life with a spouse or partner. For many, a solo life holds many attractions: peace and quiet, doing what they please, seeing whom they please, and never having to negotiate important decisions.

As those of us in the baby-boom generation cruise into our 50s, 60s, and beyond, we will need to consider what we want our lives to be like.

Important Questions About Later Life:

▶ How long should I work?

▶ Should I stay where I am or relocate?

▶ How much money do I need to retire?

▶ What are my values, interests, and goals?

▶ Who do I want to spend time with?

▶ What do I want in my "oldest old" years . . . and at the end?

These are concerns that most of us don't even think about in our early or midlife years, but they become increasingly important as we cross the age-50 milestone. Of course, these are questions that everyone must grapple with, but for single women these issues are particularly critical, because they must make them alone, and because they have far-reaching implications.

TO WORK OR NOT TO WORK

The answer to the quandary "Do I keep on working or totally retire from work?" is certainly not limited to "yes" or "no." If you are over 50, you have probably noticed that "retirement" has become the hot topic of every dinner-table conversation among your friends of both genders. Some people probably profess a desire to work indefinitely, some want to work at a different job (maybe part time) some can't wait to travel to exotic locales, others want to volunteer for their favorite charity, etc., etc.

One of the more healthy attitudes toward this issue that I see among single women is the willingness — indeed, eagerness

— to think out of the box. The issue of work is definitely not a cut-and-dried matter. There are so many options available in this arena. Here, the advantage for single women is that they can make this decision independent of anyone else's preference.

Do you want to continue working at your current career? This shouldn't be a problem, especially if you are currently employed and enjoy what you are doing. Most employers are happy to maintain their mature, knowledgeable workers. Want to scale back to part time in order to pursue some other interests? That's a great way to ease into a retirement lifestyle while still making an income and staying busy. Can't wait for that retirement party? As a woman, you probably have a substantial list of things you want to do when you no longer need that paycheck. Go for it!

HOW MUCH MONEY IS ENOUGH?

It is important for single women to understand their full financial situation. If you are good with numbers and you want to utilize one of the many excellent retirement calculators online, that may be a perfectly fine way for you to do it. If you are like the rest of us, you will want to talk to a financial adviser and let her run the numbers for you.

The average life expectancy for women today is in the low 80s. In ten years, at the rate medical science is progressing, it will probably be in the high 80s or low 90s. Today, most financial advisers are calculating our life expectancy to 103! Most of us probably won't live quite that long, but what if we do? The last thing we want to risk is running out of funds just as we really need them.

Once you understand 1) your financial position, given what you have accumulated, 2) what you will collect from Social Security, and 3) what (if any) pension or inheritance you have coming, you will be much better equipped to decide how long to work, whether you will need to relocate, and how frugal or lavish you can afford to be in your later years. If you don't have a financial adviser or financial planner already, ask your friends and colleagues for recommendations, or check out the financial-planning associations in your local area for a referral. It will cost you a few dollars for the advice, but it's money well spent. You can also check out the national Web site fpanet.org to find "a community of financial-planning experts ready to help you."

SHOULD I RELOCATE?

If you are currently living in New York City, San Francisco, Boston, or another high-cost-of-living area, your interest in moving may be primarily to lower your cost of housing. Money is certainly a valid consideration, as your money will definitely go a lot farther in rural Pennsylvania or the California Desert than it does in the big cities.

Another valid consideration is the location of your family. If you moved away from your family to pursue a career, you may be considering relocating in the future to bring you closer to your siblings or nieces and nephews. If you are a single woman with grown children, you may want to move to be nearer to your children and grandchildren.

The above points are valid reasons to consider a move, but relocating is not a trivial undertaking for a single woman. When couples move, they at least have each other, even if their new location doesn't feel like home right away — or ever. For a single person, it can be a very isolating experience. Let's look at two scenarios.

ONE WOMAN'S VIEW
MARCIA'S STORY: "I decided to live closer to my daughter"

Marcia was divorced and living alone in suburban Washington, DC. She had retired in her early 60s, mainly because her arthritis was making it increasingly difficult for her to endure the commute to her job. Initially, she enjoyed a more relaxed lifestyle and often joined one or more of her many women friends for an evening of theater, or a movie, a dinner, or just a quiet afternoon at home. Over the ensuing five years, however, Marcia watched most of her friends move away – out of the cold winters or, more often, to live near their grown children and grandchildren. Marcia's oldest child, a daughter, was married and living in northern New Jersey with her husband. "I decided to live closer to my daughter," says Marcia, "so I found a 55+ community near her and made the move."

Marcia's plan seemed sound at the time she made it, and in retrospect it was the right decision, as she now sees her daughter and her two grandchildren quite often. However, her arthritis kept her from many of the social opportunities in the community, and it took several years for her to find some true friends there. She now feels reasonably settled in New Jersey, but the move was hard on her. The adjustment period was much longer than she had bargained on and still continues today, seven years after she relocated.

Marcia's story illustrates some of the challenges of a move in later life for single women, yet it also illustrates the reasons why it may be important for some single women to relocate once the working years are over. The real question is: "Where are your connections?"

ONE WOMAN'S VIEW

SHARON'S STORY: "I like knowing I will have a core of interesting women friends with whom I can share my journey"

Sharon is divorced with no children, and still very active and healthy. She grew up on the East Coast, but when she married in her 20s, she and her husband moved to the San Francisco Bay Area for the job opportunities and the milder climate. They divorced shortly thereafter, but Sharon was already hooked on the culture, the recreational opportunities, and the beauty she saw in California. She married a second time, divorced again, and settled into a life as a well-paid professional single woman in a mid-sized Silicon Valley town.

All of Sharon's family stayed on the East Coast. Her parents are still living but are quite elderly; her brother has two daughters, but Sharon doesn't really know her nieces very well since she was not part of their lives growing up. She has saved well and will inherit some money when her parents pass on. Her financial situation is sound, and she has determined that she can retire any time now, but Sharon still enjoys her work and chooses to continue with it. She has a solid core of longtime women friends, some single, some married. She travels and attends dozens of theater productions and dinners out every year with like-minded women. She is a busy, fulfilled, and happy single woman.

Sharon has decided that she has no interest in relocating after she retires. All her friends are in the local area, and many, like her, have no children and no plans to relocate either. She says, "I like knowing I will have a core of interesting women friends with whom I can share my journey."

When she is much older, Sharon thinks she will probably sell her condo and buy into one of the growing number of continuous-care communities in her immediate area. Of course, she doesn't know how long she will live, or, for that matter, which of her friends will live a long life, but she does value companionship and knows that being part of a community will afford her the best chance of staying connected to people and finding a variety of ways to stay as mentally and physically active as possible.

Sharon's story illustrates several important decisions. She intends to continue to work as long as she enjoys it and is healthy enough to handle the physical demands and make the half-hour commute. It provides her tremendous intellectual stimulation and constitutes the purpose in her life at this time. She has decided to stay put in her condo and in her community as long as she is physically able.

Her plan to buy into a continuous-care community (CCRC) is not for everyone. It is expensive. But it can be a terrific option for single women, because it will prevent the isolation that so often befalls those aging alone in their homes. Other options for the aging journey are cooperative living and cohousing. In later life, when you are not physically able to tend to all your needs, some kind of cooperative living arrangement will keep you out of a nursing home much longer than if you lived alone.

One option I believe single women should consider, and which comes under the category of cooperative living, is home sharing. Many single, professional women own large homes or condos that may date from a time when they were married or were raising children. If that is your situation, you may want to consider inviting other like-minded women to share the space with you — kind of like *The Golden Girls* TV show of the '80s. That would mean these additional two to three women would also share the expenses involved in keeping the home maintained, inside and out. It certainly would mean a ready source of companionship and assistance when one of you needs it. This concept has its complications, but women all over the country are finding ways to manage it — legally and emotionally. If you are curious, check out the many articles online by entering "golden girls living" into your browser.

Retirement Plan Ahead **Action Steps**

As you continue to think about your retirement plan, you may want to keep the following list of action steps close by:

1 Consult Financial Professionals

See a financial planner/adviser to assess your long-term financial situation. Check out the national Web site fpanet.org to find financial-planning experts. Also, ask for referrals from friends and coworkers, then interview several advisers and select the one who most appeals to you.

2 Be Prepared

Visit an estate lawyer to create a will, a trust, and a long-term care plan that designates a decision maker in the event you cannot make decisions for yourself.

3 Home Is Where the Heart Is

Decide whether a move to a different location in the city where you currently live or to an entirely different city is the right thing for you, and weigh the pros and cons of that decision.

4 Speak with Friends

Talk to your friends about how you can age together in a fulfilling way.

5 Keep Your Family in the Loop

Let your family know of your plans and your wishes.

The concept of retirement for single women will have as many variations as there are women making plans today. One thing I have certainly learned as a retirement-transition coach is that there are really no *wrong* decisions if they are made conscientiously, just *different* choices for *different* people. This is your opportunity to create exactly the right retirement plan for *you*.

> { "There are really no *wrong* decisions if they are made conscientiously, just *different* choices for *different* people." }

INVENTING YOUR BEST RETIREMENT ... A CIRCLE OF TRUST IS A MUST

BY SUZANNE BRAUN LEVINE

One of the foremost authorities on women in the second half of life shares her thoughts on what is most important in retirement.

Suzanne Braun Levine is a writer, editor, and authority on women, families, media, and changing gender roles. Her e-book *You Gotta Have Girlfriends* continues the conversation with women in second adulthood that she celebrated in her popular books *Inventing the Rest of Our Lives, Fifty Is the New Fifty,* and *How We Love Now.* Her new e-book, *Can Men Have It All?,* examines the changing role of fatherhood and the work-life conflicts of modern couples. The first editor of *Ms.* magazine and the first woman editor of the *Columbia Journalism Review,* she is a contributor to *More* magazine and blogs for AARP, Huff/Post50, and others.

A CIRCLE OF TRUST IS A MUST

You know who your girlfriends are. I call them a "circle of trust," and as we move past 50 and many of us approach "retirement" (however we may choose to define it or live it), we count on them more than ever. Friendship is the *sine qua non* for whatever is going to work for us as we explore the rest of our lives.

Portions of this essay are adapted from *You Gotta Have Girlfriends, Fifty Is the New Fifty,* and the author's blogs.

The reasons we trust our girlfriends and love them just keep multiplying as we age:

- They are fun to be with. So much so, that they are often our first choice to celebrate important milestones with — like a 50th birthday, a new job, or retirement.
- They root for us, and they put up with us.
- They stand up for us, and they stand by us.
- They listen sympathetically when we need to vent.
- They know when we are hurt or angry and how to patch things up.
- They make us laugh and keep us sane.

While researching my book *You Gotta Have Girlfriends*, I found new studies of all kinds that showed how having girlfriends in your life reduces stress, enhances pleasure, and even strengthens the immune system. We live better, longer, healthier, and happier lives when we are linked with other women in a circle of trust.

> "Having girlfriends in your life reduces stress, enhances pleasure, and even strengthens the immune system."

For many of us, those girlfriends came into our lives through the work we did — frequently at jobs that wouldn't have been open to us before we changed the world. And as we ask ourselves the questions, *"What will I do with the rest of my life?"* and *"What's next?"* our girlfriends become more important than ever.

It was the collaborative effort at *Ms.* magazine, where I worked for over 15 years, that created the friendships that sustain me now. Having worked in the Women's Movement, I have had a taste of what it feels like to participate in changing the world, but almost any woman who grew up in those years can also recall a day or a moment when she understood that life was different than it had been before.

Over the past 40 years, our generation has built quite a track record of blazing new trails. And as women move past 50, we reach the height of our powers; we don't care what other people think, and we know very well what *we* think. And, of course, we have a secret weapon: our girlfriends.

Changing the world is something we do very well. I would like to propose one more group activity: *inventing our best retirement.*

THE ENCORE MOVEMENT

For many of us, the most important aspect of working, aside from money, is community. If work contributes mightily to our identity, we want to find ways for retirement to do the same. That may mean retiring from one job but moving to another. And for our generation, there is good news. It is easier than ever before to find like-minded women and organizations that nurture our desire for community and change.

I am working in a new, exhilarating, social-justice movement spearheaded by the nonprofit Encore.org, which focuses on mobilizing the untapped and disrespected potential of people in the second half of life who want to make a vital contribution to society. If this sounds and feels like a continuation of the efforts to redefine the role of women, you're right. The Encore movement is about redefining the roles for *all* of us as we age.

The Encore spirit also answers an impulse that comes with age — to give back. The closet-cleaning itch we all recognize is really a metaphor for divesting ourselves of the superficial and petty and investing ourselves in the important things in life. In the process of contemplating the big picture, we come to think about what our achievements and failures have been and what our legacy will be. *What really matters to us? How have we changed the world?*

Part of this new movement and stage also involves connecting with organizations we've come to know and trust, like the AARP, and new ones that help empower, inspire, guide, and sustain us. We are joining organizations like The Transition Network, communities of professional women who are coming together to seek new opportunities and friendships in chapters around the country; and we are creating communities online like the WHOA! Network, which seeks to make women more visible at every age, but especially as we age. There are so many possibilities that are available to us now. We have reached a critical mass. The breakthroughs we have achieved and the networks we have established are fostering an interdependence that empowers all of us.

As we contemplate our own retirement, we can look to other women as horizontal role models on this journey and count on the support of our girlfriends. Whether reaching out across the globe to help others or finding a network in our communities to support our next project, we know that with a circle of trust, we don't have to go it alone.

> "Empowerment is a team sport. Every one of us who is making change and taking risks in her own life is on the team."

A NEW GOLDEN RULE

It is time for a New Golden Rule. Gloria Steinem says, "Do unto yourself as you have been doing unto others." I would add to that, "Do unto yourself as you would do unto your friends."

> *"Many think of courage . . . as a solitary journey. We believe the journey of courage is best walked with women friends who literally and figuratively 'en-courage' us."*

—Deborah Collins Stephens, Jackie Speier, Michaelene Cristini Risley, and Jan Yanehiro, friends and coauthors of *This Is Not the Life I Ordered*.

> *"There are times when a friend provides more than the warm soup of empathy. She becomes a catalyst for change. Over a long life, full of disruptions, stops, and start-ups, friends can be the collaborators, the instigators who make change possible."*

—Ellen Goodman and Patricia O'Brien, *I Know Just What You Mean*

· RESOURCES ·

Help for what's next . . . trusted advisers and resources.

- Encore.org — *Second acts for the greater good.*
  Investing in people who are using the second half of
  their lives to change the world.
  encore.org

- AARP — *Real possibilities.* Helping people 50 and older
  improve the quality of their lives.
  aarp.org

- The Transition Network — *Embracing change after 50.*
  An inclusive community of professional women.
  thetransitionnetwork.org

- NextAvenue — *Where grown-ups keep growing.*
  America is in the midst of an age boom and with it, an
  amazing transition.
  nextavenue.org

- Huff/Post50 — *Life begins at 50.* The best blogs and
  conversation on topics that matter most to baby
  boomers.
  huffingtonpost.com/50

- Feisty Side of Fifty/Baby Boomer Women —
  Celebrating women 50 and better. We're totally
  transforming the spirit and style of aging.
  feistysideoffifty.com

- WHOA! Network — *Women honoring our age.*
  Reinventing what it means to grow older and to believe
  we should be seen and heard through all our life stages.
  whoanetwork.com

Retirement Plan Ahead **Action Steps**

Taking practical and emotional responsibility for the rest of your life includes managing your checkbook and your health care, but it also includes healing the past, revising life patterns, and responding in the best way you can to what every day brings. Here are important questions to answer as you contemplate your retirement years:

1 How Long Do You Plan to Work?

Do you know whether you have the choice? Do you want to change the kind of work you do? If so, will you need training? How would your answers be different if your circumstances changed from being a partner to being alone — or vice versa?

2 How Much Money Will You Need?

Do you know how to go about figuring this out? If not, do you know where to go for help? What sources will that "paycheck" come from? If you currently don't have an adequate nest egg, what can you do between now and whenever?

3 Where Will You Want to Live?

How do you want to live — alone or with others (friends, family, like-minded contemporaries)? And how does that situation compare with your current one?

4 Have You Got Your Safety Nets in Place?

What kind of care (insurance, trusted advisers, support group) have you provided for yourself?

5 Have You Made Your Wishes Known?

What kind of care or support do you want to provide for dependents? What provisions have you made to ensure that your medical directives are on record?

DITCH RETIREMENT! INSTEAD, GRADUATE INTO AN ENCORE CAREER

BY MARCI ALBOHER

A well-known expert in the field of encore careers describes a new way of thinking about the years traditionally "consumed" by retirement.

Marci Alboher is a leading authority on the changing face of work and a vice president at Encore.org, a nonprofit organization whose mission is to make it easier for millions of people to pursue encore careers — "second acts for the greater good." She is a former blogger and columnist for the *New York Times* and author of *The Encore Career Handbook: How to Make a Living and a Difference in the Second Half of Life* (Workman Publishing, 2013).

MAKING A DIFFERENCE

I first heard about encore careers in 2007. I was a workplace columnist for the *New York Times* when I interviewed Marc Freedman, who had just published the book *Encore: Finding Work That Matters in the Second Half of Life*. That book introduced me to a big new idea — that many people hitting midlife are seized with the urge to make a difference in the world, and that legions of them are going through some kind of reinvention to do it. With more than 75 million baby boomers, and thousands turning 50 and 60 every day, that's a huge reservoir of talent available to fix our broken schools, preserve our threatened environment, and solve so many of our nagging social problems. Imagine if even a small fraction of this cohort scrapped the idea of retirement and instead focused on moving into encore careers — second acts for the greater good.

I was so intrigued by this vision of an army of late-career do-gooders that I wrote several follow-up pieces on it. The issue hit me both professionally and personally. I had lived through a big career change myself, having abandoned corporate law to become a journalist when I was in my 30s. That shift was motivated by wanting more purpose in my life.

In 2008, not long after first writing about the encore idea, I faced yet another career upheaval, only this time it wasn't my choice. The *New York Times* abruptly canceled my "Shifting Careers" column and blog; though both were extremely popular, I was an expensive freelancer, and the media industry was trying to figure out its own survival. I was blindsided. After all, I was tweeting. I was on the cutting edge. I was also devastated and embarrassed. I was a *workplace expert* who was now *out of a job*.

Eventually, I networked my way back to Marc Freedman, the author of that *Encore* book that had so affected me. And in time, I joined the staff of Encore.org, the small nonprofit he founded that is spearheading the idea of encore careers as a solution to our greatest social problems. I now spend my days working on ways to help more people move into encore careers.

> "Many people hitting midlife are seized with the urge to make a difference in the world."

Marci Alboher

ADVICE FOR THE PATH AHEAD

In the past four years, I've interviewed hundreds of people who have embarked on encore careers — and that work culminated in my writing *The Encore Career Handbook*, which was published in early 2013.

After the book's release, I spent the better part of a year traveling the country on a national tour. I spoke at bookstores, libraries, college reunions, and even a graduation ceremony. But it wasn't your typical graduation. The students were a group of people in their 50s who'd just completed Encore! Hartford, a University of Connecticut program designed to help seasoned corporate professionals transition into managerial positions in the nonprofit sector.

As I looked out into the audience, I was struck by the sight of a group of middle-aged people lining up for diplomas, while their supportive families — often in the form of teenage children — cheered them on. In preparing for this unique graduation speech, I scoured the Internet for commencement speeches aimed at typical college graduates. I watched and read many powerful talks: Oprah at Harvard, Arianna Huffington at Smith College, Stephen Colbert at the University of Virginia, and Meryl Streep at Barnard. And in doing so, I realized that the kind of advice they were giving to 20-year-olds had a lot in common with the tips I wanted to give to a group of 50-year-olds repurposing themselves for purpose-oriented second and third acts. Whether you're planning to start an encore career in the immediate future or closer to your retirement years, I'd like to share with you some of the ideas I included in my commencement address at Encore! Hartford:

THINGS TO KEEP IN MIND, PART 1

- **Recognize that your journey is just beginning.** You may not have discovered the work you were meant to do, but you have the goods to get there.

- **Expect a lot of wrong turns and detours.** Getting lost is how you find your way.

- **Failure is a necessary stop on the way to where you're meant to go.** Or as Oprah recently said at Harvard, "Failure is just life trying to move us in another direction."

- **Your network will take you where you need to go.** The most important assets you have are the relationships you've built up over the course of your years of experience — at work, in your community, and wherever those years took you.

Thinking ahead to what I like to call the "encore" years means being realistic about the changes that are bound to occur. We are all quite familiar with the things that diminish with age — like the ability to remember names and read tiny print on menus, or a vision of yourself as physically invincible. But there are also a whole lot of things that actually get better with age. And those will be the building blocks of a successful encore career.

THINGS TO KEEP IN MIND, PART 2

- **Empathy and emotional stability.** With age comes a greater ability to listen and hear the concerns of others. Which is why people in midlife make wonderful coaches, social workers, counselors, spiritual leaders, mentors, and advisers. I stopped counting the number of people who've told me they'd never want to see a therapist who's under 40.

- **Wisdom.** How many times have you wished that you knew then what you know now? Truth is, wisdom only arrives with accumulated years. Go out and use it!

- **Leadership.** It's no accident that heads of state and the hallways of Congress are filled with people over 60. As we age, our ability to lead and synthesize ideas gets stronger.

Even with all of these attributes, you'll need to adopt the right mindset in order to get this encore thing right. So . . .

ADVICE AS YOU CONSIDER YOUR ENCORE CAREER

- **Give yourself permission to get lost.** You still have time to experiment, to take a few detours, and to invest in yourself.

- **Embrace lifelong learning.** Education used to be front-loaded at the beginning of life. But in the new world order, we need to repeatedly fill the tank. If you're going to work another 20 years, know that the best investment you may be able to make is in your own skills and training. Don't be surprised if you're back in school before too long.

- **Be aware of ageism, but don't fixate on it.** Look for fields and work environments where experience is valued. Become a master at intergenerational mentoring and finding the upsides to working with — and for — younger people. And take every opportunity to defy stereotypes about aging by embracing new technology and new ways of working. There is no age limit on changing the world. And only when more people move into encore careers will stereotypes of older workers fade.

- **Meaningful work isn't all sunshine and rainbows.** Ask any teacher, activist, or nonprofit executive director. Doing good work doesn't always feel good. You will likely still run into your fair share of difficult colleagues, bureaucracies, and bad days.

Retirement **Action Steps**

Here are five action steps to help you get started on your way toward your encore career:

1 Carve Out Space and Time

Before you take any specific actions, commit to giving yourself the proper space and time to figure out what you want and how you're going to get there. Set aside some time and honor it. It can be as little as one lunch a week, your morning walk, or half a day each weekend, or as much as a weeklong retreat or even a gap year. Once you carve out the time, you can then focus on what you'll do to use it productively.

2 Take Inventory

Traditional retirement planning involves surveying whether you're prepared for what's next. So does encore planning. You'll want to look at each piece of your life and start envisioning what you'd like it to look like going forward, from your home to your finances, to whether you want to work for pay in the next stage of your life, and what kinds of things interest you the most.

3 Get Out of Your Head and Into the World

Once you start getting a picture (even a fuzzy one) of what's attracting you, start to do some experimenting. The best way to start is by volunteering or doing some pro-bono consulting. With each experiment, focus on a few things. Building your network. Finding ways to use your skills and experiences to maximum impact. And most important, identify whether the skills you're using and the issues you're working on are the ones you want to immerse in further in your encore career.

4 Find Your Fellow Travelers

All transitions are easier when you have a support team. Spend some time thinking of who's going to help you on this journey. For some people, a good friend, colleague, or even romantic partner makes sense. Others find it valuable to find people a bit outside of their daily life. Consider forming an encore transition group so that you can stay connected to others who are also interested in moving into encore careers.

5 Invest in Your Skills

If you haven't made a big change in a long time, it's likely that the world has changed a lot since the last time you had to present yourself for new opportunities. It's also possible that your interests may take you in a wildly different direction from where you are now. Embrace the chance to give yourself a skills-and-education makeover, so that you are the best version of yourself as you figure out where to make your mark.

These steps, along with new skills you acquire and a positive attitude, are all going to help you as you embark on whatever new work you choose as your encore. Instead of settling for the old definition of retirement, you can be a trailblazer. You can take on the project of reinventing yourself to make sure that you have the skills and connections to make a difference in the world during the extended working lives we are all lucky enough to enjoy. But don't think it will be easy. The really worthwhile things never are.

As you work on your own encore transition, keep in mind that you are part of something far bigger than your own reinvention. If the pioneers of the encore movement get this right, we have the power to leave the world in far better shape than we found it. And that's a legacy we can pass down to future generations.

HOW TO REINVENT YOUR CAREER FOR SEMI-RETIREMENT

BY NANCY COLLAMER, M.S.

A prominent career coach and author shares advice on how to plan for a fun, flexible, and fulfilling semi-retirement career.

Nancy Collamer is a career coach, speaker, and author of *Second-Act Careers: 50+ Ways to Profit from Your Passions During Semi-Retirement*. She writes a semimonthly column about careers for NextAvenue.org (PBS) and Forbes.com. Nancy holds an M.S. in Career Development from the College of New Rochelle and a B.A. in Psychology from UNC/Chapel Hill. You can connect with Nancy on her Web site at mylifestylecareer.com or on Twitter @NancyCollamer.

DON'T RETIRE, REINVENT!

Welcome, in advance, to your second-act career! Even if you're still only in your 40s or 50s, it's never too early to begin thinking about options for working during retirement. A second-act career can provide you with an opportunity to finally do work you really love — and the sooner you begin to explore, the more time you'll have to research, evaluate, and test out possibilities.

{ "A second–act career can provide you with an opportunity to finally do work you really love." }

Your Plan of Attack

The first step in gearing up to work during retirement is to spend time thinking about what you love to do, have the ability or aptitude to do well, and find meaningful. There are many methodologies available to help you discern new career goals: assessments, personality quizzes, and self-inventories. But sometimes the best way to create those "aha" moments of self-discovery is simply to ponder your responses to thought-provoking questions. Here are some to help you get the ball rolling:

Reinvention Questions to Ponder

▶ What do you want to spend your days talking about?

▶ What is the one thing you feel extremely qualified to teach other people?

▶ What political, global, community, or spiritual issues are most important to you?

▶ What is something that you find easy that others find difficult?

▶ What are some problems or challenges in your community or the wider marketplace that you'd like to help fix?

▶ What did you love to do as a child?

▶ What do you dream about doing (no matter how far-fetched)?

▶ Whose job would you love to have? Why?

▶ What can't you stop yourself from doing?

{ "Need another reason to embrace working in retirement? According to a study of nearly half a million people in France, people who delay retirement have less risk of developing Alzheimer's disease and other types of dementia." }

EXPLORING YOUR OPTIONS

Knowing your strengths, interests, and talents is critical to crafting a fulfilling second-act career. But it is not enough to focus only on what is important to you. After all, if there is no ready market for your services or products, then it will be impossible to turn your passions into profits, no matter how motivated you may be.

That's why the next step in this process is to research the new world of semi-retirement options. As you begin to explore, you'll discover that people are now earning income in ways that we never could have imagined just a few short years ago: selling on the Internet, self-publishing books on demand, and teaching Webinars online. Jobs we aspired to when we were younger have become obsolete, and new careers — like virtual assistants, app designers, social-media consultants, and bloggers — have filled the void.

Here are some places to get your research started:

Career Research Resources

- Attend an industry conference or expo
- Review college catalogs to discover new fields of interest

- Sign up for an adult-education course at your local community college

- Visit the U.S. Department of Labor sites: America's CareerInfoNet (acinet.org) and The Occupational Outlook Handbook (onetcenter.org)

- Consult Fabjob.com for downloadable guides to a wide variety of entrepreneurial ideas

· RESOURCES ·

Here are some Web sites where you can get inspired by second-act career stories:

- Huff/Post50 (huffingtonpost.com/50) The section on the popular *Huffington Post* Web site that features blogs targeted to boomers.

- Life Reimagined (lifereimagined.aarp.org) A site run by AARP to help boomers navigate and reimagine change midlife.

- Next Avenue (nextavenue.org) A PBS-affiliated Web site with advice and resources for boomers.

- Pivot Planet (pivotplanet.com) Connects people looking to change careers with expert advisers working in different fields.

ONE WOMAN'S VIEW

MY STORY: "Don't throw out the baby with the bathwater"

Shortly before giving birth to my first child, I decided I wanted to leave my job as a director of Human Resources and find a more lifestyle-friendly way to earn an income. At the time, I played around with all sorts of ideas: one day I wanted to be a nutritionist, and the next a fashion designer.

For months, my husband listened patiently to my "brainstorms of the day." But finally he said, "Honey, I'll support whatever decision you make. But why don't you focus on something at least remotely connected to Human Resources? It's what you know. You've already invested a lot of time and energy in that field. Isn't there something you can do with that?"

At the time, his suggestion irritated me. But as much as I hated to admit it, my husband was right. He wasn't saying I had to stay in Human Resources — he was simply suggesting that I be open to alternatives that better leveraged my hard-earned education and experience.

And you know what? Upon reflection, I realized that there were parts of my career that I did find rewarding: I loved mentoring younger employees, talking about career planning, and doing public speaking. And even though the coaching piece had been only a small part of my responsibilities, I discovered that with additional training I could easily leverage that experience into a coaching business.

So even if you are determined, like I was, to move as far as possible from your corporate identity, don't be so quick to "throw out the baby with the bathwater." There are always pieces of your previous work experience — no matter how seemingly insignificant — that are worth using as the foundational pieces of your second act.

Retirement Plan Ahead **Action Steps**

1 Envision the Life You Want

When you think back to the last time you planned your career (junior year in college?), it's likely that your decisions were based more on practical concerns, like paying the rent and putting food on the table, than on your personal hopes and dreams. But now it is time to switch things up. Instead of allowing your career to dominate your life, it's time for your life to take center stage. Think about the role you want work to play in your life: *How many hours do you want to work? Do you want to run your own business? What type of balance do you want to strike between work, family, community, play, and self?* Once you've defined the type of life you want to lead, it will be far easier to focus in on the types of businesses and part-time careers that will best support your lifestyle goals.

2 Look to Your Past for Clues to Your Future

Is there some aspect of your work experiences — no matter how seemingly insignificant — that might be worth leveraging as a bridge into your next act? Perhaps you excelled at planning budgets and event management; that's a skill that you could transfer into working as a director for a nonprofit. Or maybe you loved mentoring younger workers at your company — a passion that could be turned into a second act as an executive coach. Remember: all things being equal, it will be easiest to create a second-act career that is at least partially related to what you did before.

3 Don't Get Hung Up on Trying to Find Your "One and Only" Passion

Few people have one driving passion, and the focus on building a second act around that "one true love" can create needless anxiety and frustration. But that doesn't mean that introspection is time wasted; think about causes you find compelling, people you find interesting, and activities you enjoy and find meaningful — and then start exploring career options that line up with those varied interests and skills.

4 Adopt an Opportunity-Seeker Mind-Set

Never before in history have we enjoyed easier access to more information — you can learn about thousands, even millions, of new options for semi-retirement from newspapers, television, and the Internet. Many of the people profiled in my book, *Second-Act Careers*, found rewarding new paths simply by keeping their "opportunity antenna" on alert and paying closer attention to what they were reading, hearing, and experiencing on a daily basis.

5 Set Up a Personal Reinvention Research and Development (R&D) Budget

Put aside a small amount of money each year to spend on classes, workshops, and other venues that will help you to learn about and train for potential new career directions. It doesn't need to be much, but once you earmark those funds, you'll be more likely to invest in your ongoing education (and if you hesitate to spend the money on yourself, just think about what you've spent on your kids' piano lessons over the years!). Adult education is a big business these days, and there are more opportunities than ever for people of all ages to indulge in lifelong learning.

5 Don't Go It Alone

One of the biggest problems I see when people try to change their careers is that they feel like they need to go it alone. But when you think back to other major transitions in your life — graduations, marriage, or new jobs — chances are that you had a network of friends, family, and mentors who guided and supported you through the process. Surrounding yourself with a supportive community is a critical part of career-reinvention success. It will help keep you focused, accountable, and moving forward on your journey.

TRAVEL – THE GIFT THAT CONTINUES TO GIVE

BY AKAISHA KADERLI

An internationally recognized expert on travel in retirement provides a road map to planning the perfect getaways.

Recognized retirement expert Akaisha Kaderli defies conventional life descriptions and prefers active trailblazing instead. Financially independent at the age of 38, she and her husband have been traveling the globe since 1991 and were promoting medical tourism before the phrase was invented. They often find themselves on the cutting edge of societal trends and love sharing that expansive view in their books and on their Web site, RetireEarlyLifestyle.com.

MEETING CHALLENGES

When many people think of retirement, they picture fabulous getaways and unique adventures in exotic places. If you have caught yourself dreaming of painting in Italy, taking a cooking course in France, visiting national parks throughout the United States, or engaging with the Maya in Central America, but you don't know how to start, you're in luck. . . .

I'm a world traveler, and I'm here to help.

BEGIN NOW — BECOME PAPERLESS

If you're planning to do a lot of traveling in your future, the first thing you want to do is to become paperless as soon as possible. Begin this process now — *before* your retirement and all those fun trips you've been fantasizing about. Get rid of junk mail, cancel hard-copy magazine and newspaper subscriptions, and give up those deliveries of wine and specialty coffees.

Arrange for all your bank and brokerage statements to be sent to you electronically. Ask for this to be done with your credit-card bills as well, and set up payment of bills with an online service such as BillPay. Set up multiple debit cards with different accounts, and do the same for two credit cards, so that you have a more secure way to access funds abroad.

> "Make sure as much paperwork as possible is available to you online."

Prepare to take care of your tax information digitally. Make the choice to work with a CPA who will do electronic filing, or prepare your own tax reports through TurboTax.

Make sure as much paperwork as possible is available to you online. Having physical papers will tether you to your home or will require you to pay someone to monitor your mail and to send you paperwork that may need your signature. It's an unnecessary hardship, so cut that out of your equation right away.

Of course, if you anticipate going on short trips, you can just stop your mail and pick it up when you return. But if you're thinking about doing a lot of extended travel, arrange for your domicile to be in a tax-friendly state and utilize the assistance of mail forwarding. There are services like Earth Class Mail, which will scan your first-class mail so you know what might need attention, and it can be forwarded to your current location if necessary.

COST CONTROL

Transportation and housing abroad represent your two highest travel expenses — whether you take mini trips or you live your life on the road. You must decide if you will be taking short journeys over long weekends, a week or two at a time, or whether or not you want to have more of an open calendar. As a matter of fact, the longer your travel itinerary, the more transportation and housing options open up for you.

Shorter trips mean you will be caring for — and paying for — both housing at home and housing on the road. You will also need to financially cover your vehicle at home and your transportation needs while on the road.

Longer trips of several months or more will allow you to take advantage of opportunities for fabulous accommodations, whether it's on a repositioning cruise or house sitting or house swapping. If you are gone for long periods, you could choose to sell your car or place it on storage status, thereby controlling your costs of transportation and upkeep.

TRANSPORTATION

We chose to be car free years ago, and life has never been easier. We don't rent cars in our travel locations, except when we're in the U.S., and we don't own a car in a foreign country. Owning a car abroad makes you subject to theft; the need for repairs, maintenance, licensing, and insurance; and a whole host of other concerns, like needing to find a parking space when you shop, go to a restaurant, or stay in a hotel.

Use local transportation or a bicycle whenever possible, and if you're not near a popular route, hire a driver for the hour, the day, or the week. This service is far cheaper abroad than it is in the U.S. or Canada. Taxis can be placed on retainer, and for a couple of dollars they will pick you up, wait for you, and then take you back. Many will bring your groceries into your kitchen at your request, should you be dealing with stairs or a big day of shopping. The cost of taxis is far cheaper than the expense of owning a car.

Public transportation is widely available in Latin America, Europe, and Asia. Having your own vehicle to worry about will limit you in a number of ways. For example, if you go sailing across a lake for a few days, you'll need to park your car unattended overnight. If you are traveling with your own vehicle and stopping in different places each night, then you must unload your belongings each evening and load them each morning, unless you have access to locked interior parking. While traveling, it is unwise to park on the streets overnight with valuable items packed in your car.

SWAP YOUR HOME?

Decide whether you want to keep your house or to sell it. Retaining your home means that you will still be responsible for maintenance, insurance, and repairs, but it will put you in a perfect position to house swap. House swapping will also allow you to keep your pets safely at home and have your gardens tended, as each person swapping will be caring for the other's belongings.

You could rent your home out, but this is a personal choice. If you are very attached to your possessions and you rent your house out, the gardens might not be the same when you return, and chances are you will need to provide care for your pet, which is another expense.

REPOSITIONING CRUISES

Twice a year, in the spring and in the fall, cruise ships are "repositioned" to different ports to sail itineraries that are most popular during those seasons. Since cruise lines do not want ships to sail empty, you will find some of the best deals during this time. On repositioning cruises, your discount may be 30 to 70 percent off what you'd pay for a regular cruise! Since these cruises are usually longer in duration than typical cruises, they're perfect for retirees who have more time to travel.

> "On repositioning cruises, your discount may be 30 to 70 percent off what you'd pay for a regular cruise!"

The most sought-after autumn repositioning cruises are those from Europe to the Caribbean, or from Alaska to the Caribbean through the Panama Canal. But you'll find that some cruise ships also sail to Asia from the Mediterranean by going through the Suez Canal, while others cross the Atlantic to South America. In the spring, this shifting of positions occurs in reverse.

If your calendar is fairly open and you want to get from one continent to another, this is an affordable way to do so. You will save money on transportation, you'll get to see exotic ports — *and* you won't have to worry about suffering from jet lag.

ONE WOMAN'S VIEW
CLAIRE'S STORY: "Planning the trip of a lifetime"

Claire, who had lived most of her adult life in the Northeastern United States, had wanted to return to Italy since her college days. She had spent her middle years focused on career and family, but now that she was retired she was planning the trip of a lifetime.

Having earlier joined a house-sitting Web site, she utilized her rusty Italian to make arrangements to care for a beautiful home just outside Naples, Italy, for two months. The owners were planning a trip to England and wanted someone to care for their small dog.

Now, she just had to get to Naples.

She had been hearing of repositioning cruises, and this was the perfect opportunity for her. It was soon to be spring, so Claire knew that cruise ships would be leaving New York City and going to the Mediterranean. Visiting the Web site RepositioningCruise.com, she checked out her options. Feeling a bit overwhelmed, she arranged to speak with a repositioning-cruise specialist at their 800 number. She learned that there was a cruise that would take her to Capri, Italy, and that she could easily take a train from there to Naples. Since she had called months before the cruise was set to sail, she'd have a better choice of cabin selection. When the specialist told her she would be saving 50 percent off what she would otherwise pay for a regular in-season cruise, she was delighted. That seemed like icing on the cake!

Taking a couple of weeks to cross the ocean, Claire was concerned that she might be bored, but the specialist assured her there was always something to do. Lectures, games, shows, a casino, bars, and specialty restaurants were all available, as were a good gym and spa. She also found out she could obtain cash for port shopping on board the ship through an ATM.

Knowing that her travel itinerary was set, Claire was now able to sit back, relax, and begin planning what she would pack for her summer in Italy!

Retirement Plan Ahead **Action Steps**

As a seasoned traveler, you'll be exposed to different cultures and languages. It's one of the most exciting lifestyles available. Whether you journey through exotic lands or cross-country to see family and friends, travel is a gift you give yourself — and it's a gift that keeps on giving!

1 Go Paperless

If you're going to be doing a lot of traveling in retirement, go paperless sooner rather than later. For example, subscribe only to online newspapers and magazines. Arrange for your bank and brokerage statements to be received online. Have your credit-card bills available digitally and establish a way to pay bills with an online service such as BillPay. Set up more than one debit card with different accounts and do the same for two credit cards, for a more secure way to access funds abroad.

2 Tax Time

Prepare to take care of your tax information digitally. Make the choice to work with a CPA who will do electronic filing, or prepare your own tax reports through TurboTax.

3 Avoid Mountains of Mail

Before you leave for any extended vacation, stop your mail and then pick it up when you return. Or arrange for your domicile to be in a tax-friendly state and utilize the assistance of mail forwarding.

4 What to Do About Home and Car

Before setting off to explore the world in retirement, decide on your housing and transportation options. For example, will you sell or rent out your home? Do a home exchange or try house sitting? Sell your car or put it in storage and use public transportation and/or a bicycle abroad?

5 Research Web Sites

Check out these useful sites online:

- Fidelity.com for BillPay and debit/credit cards
- worldnomads.com and journals.worldnomads.com/language-guides for traveler's insurance and free language apps
- turbotax.com
- RetireEarlyLifestyle.com/travelhousing and RetireEarlyLifestyle.com/singletraveler
- Skype.com for cheap/free worldwide communication with video and magicJack.com for cheap phone calling to the U.S. and Canada
- EarthClassMail.com

PLANNING A BACKPACK-
AND-A-ROLLIE RETIREMENT

BY NANCY THOMPSON

**A master at frugal traveling reveals how to see the
world in retirement – without breaking the bank.**

Nancy Thompson is a travel writer and lifestyle blogger sharing her
adventures of retirement, shoestring travel, and living the good life
wherever the road or her frequent-flyer miles takes her. Her passion
for travel and research has made Nancy a go-to resource for ideas,
information, and inspiration on living your retirement-travel dreams.
Her blog is justabackpackandarollie.com.

BECOMING A "VAGABOND RETIREE"

Maybe you were one of those 20-year-old free spirits who
stuffed everything they could into an oversized backpack and
set out to see the world before you settled down. Or maybe,
like most of us, you only dreamed about that kind of travel
and then stepped straight onto the well-worn path already
laid out for you — work, marriage, kids. Your travel dreams
were put on the shelf, and after a few years, you made a trip
with the backpack — to drop it off at your local Goodwill. A
big adventure became a week at Disney World. It's funny how
that happens.

But our dreams never really go away.

What I know for sure is that sometime between 40 and 50, those old dreams start to resurface. Gone for a while, but not forgotten. That travel gypsy is still alive and well. A little older, a lot wiser, and eager to explore the world.

Don't worry, there's still time.

A growing number of people are becoming "vagabond retirees." People in their 50s, 60s, and 70s are packing up their new, high-tech backpacks and heading out to become citizens of the world.

Want to join them? It's easy. And it doesn't have to blow your hard-earned retirement nest egg either.

> "Traveling on a retiree budget does require thinking outside the box."

Traveling on a retiree budget does require thinking outside the box, lots of research, some advance planning, a sense of adventure, and a willingness to be flexible. Don't wait until you are officially retired to set your travel dreams in motion. Include them in your planning now. Read the next section for a few simple ideas that will help you get started.

WELCOME TO TRAVEL PLANNING 101

Create a Travel Dream Board. It might sound hokey, but it's fun, it's easy, and it works! Buy a large piece of poster board, gather up lots of magazines, travel brochures, and old photos, and get scissors and a glue stick. It's as simple as cutting out pictures and pasting them onto the board. Don't overthink this. Cut out everything that catches your eye — beach sunsets, different cultures, village life, bustling cities, historical settings, or mountain views — anything that inspires your wanderlust. Can you see yourself in the picture? Then it belongs on your board. I call this visual goal setting. If you want, you can do this online by going to Pinterest and creating your personal travel board. Check out the getaway images that others are pinning on their boards.

Make a Wish List. Use the images on your Travel Dream Board to create a Wish List. Here's where you get more specific. What are your must-haves for a travel or retirement-living destination? Do you prefer a sleepy village or a bustling city? The beach or mountains? Easy access or remote? The options are endless, but honing this list to your top five or six major preferences will give you a great jumping-off point for your initial research.

Do your research. Whether you need to find out about the best small hotels or hostels while backpacking through Central America, fabulous house swaps in France, or the kind of visa you need to make a trek across Tibet, the information is all available on the Internet. With a little research and perseverance, you'll locate where the best airports are, what ground transportation is cheap and easy, who speaks English in the country you're going to, and what currency is used there.

Become an armchair traveler. Read and use the country and city travel guides from Rick Steves and Lonely Planet. Check out books from your local library to learn about the adventures of other travelers (so you benefit from their experience and avoid their mistakes). Reading about how someone bought and fixed up a run-down farm in Portugal or walked all 500 miles of the Camino de Santiago can be very inspiring and educational.

Get connected. Find and connect with the folks who are blazing the trail ahead of you. Ask questions and get the scoop from people who have been there, done that. It's helpful to know the good, the bad, and the "never again" about a place before you go. Start reading travel blogs. Many are filled with firsthand information, great personal stories, and links to more resources.

Retirement travel doesn't have to mean package tours, luxury cruises, or high-ticket hotels. My experience as a frugal traveler, taking just a backpack and a rollie, has taught me that you can save a lot of money and have a much richer time if you live more like a local and less like a tourist.

LIVE LIKE A LOCAL — SLEEP HERE

Housing will probably be your biggest travel expense. The following options will not only save you money, but allow you to really connect with a location:

WWOOFing: World Wide Opportunities on Organic Farms. Volunteers trade farm duties for room and board. Accommodations are simple and the work can be hard at times, but if the chance to harvest grapes in Italy, learn how to make goat cheese in France, or get your hands dirty on an organic herb garden in New Zealand appeals to you, then WWOOFing is the way to go. A surprising number of people in their 50s, 60s, and beyond are signing up. wwoofusa.org

Hosteling: If you were a backpacking 20-something, you probably remember hostels as cheap, dorm-style rooms with bunk beds and rented sheets, a bath down the hall, and a party-hardy crowd. Not a gray hair in sight. They weren't called youth hostels for nothing. Much has changed. Nowadays, more than 15 percent of hostelers are over 50, and the number is growing. Offering private rooms with baths, online booking, fresh and free linens, and more, today's hostels are catering to the mature traveler on a budget. Two things about hosteling have not changed: they are still inexpensive and a wonderful way to meet other travelers. hihostels.com

Workamping: For some folks, hitting the road in a motor home is at the top of their retirement wish list. But it's not as cheap as you might think. When you budget for gas and campground fees, you could pay more to park your RV than you would for a moderately priced hotel room. One unique and fun way to make your RV travel more affordable is by becoming a workamper. Through such Web sites as Workamper News (workampernews.com) and Camp Host (camphost.org), travelers can find and apply for thousands of seasonal and year-round jobs. Many RVers work during the summer season as camp hosts, collecting fees from campers, directing them to available sites, answering questions, and watching for problems. In return, they receive a free campsite and often a small stipend.

House Sitting: Short- and long-term house-sitting opportunities are available worldwide through online sites like House Carers (housecarers.com) and Trusted House Sitters (trustedhousesitters.com). Most house-sitting jobs involve some form of pet care and modest home maintenance, like watering the plants and bringing in the mail. Homeowners feel secure that their home is occupied and taken care of in their absence. You get a great place to stay for free and the chance to live like a local. It's a win-win situation.

A FEW MORE MONEY-SAVING TIPS

Make sure your credit card has mileage benefits. Use it wisely, but use it. Those points add up and will save you thousands on airfare.

Persevere. Airline prices fluctuate daily, but in general the best deals go to those who are patient and diligent. Travel pros say that, according to statistics, those who book early in the morning or late at night, especially on Saturdays and Wednesdays, find the best deals.

Lower-price guarantee. Most U.S. airlines (but not all) have a guaranteed airfare clause buried in the fine print that says if you purchase a ticket and the price drops, they will refund the difference. Sites like Yapta.com can track airline fares and notify you if a price drops.

Travel off-season. You will save on both your airfare and hotel. When the tourists leave and properties or seats on a flight are empty, prices drop. It's the law of supply and demand. This applies to home rentals as well. Many off-season prices are negotiable. People would rather rent their apartment to you for 30 percent off than leave it vacant. Never hesitate to ask.

ONE WOMAN'S VIEW
MY HOUSE-SITTING STORY:
"Two glorious weeks on Vancouver Island"

Recently, my husband and I spent two glorious weeks in summer on Vancouver Island in a beautiful, art-filled home, just a five-minute walk from a provincial park with miles of hiking trails and a five-minute drive to the waterfront town of Sydney. Two weeks in a hotel would have cost us at least $1,500–$2,000, but our stay was absolutely free because we were house sitting. In return for my daily watering of a lush garden, bringing in the mail, and retrieving the newspaper, we luxuriated in the comforts of our temporary home, which included harvesting all of the fresh fruits and veggies we could eat. We could not have had an easier or richer experience.

Retirement Plan Ahead Action Steps

1 Dare to Dream

Start with your Travel Dream Board and Wish List. These two exercises will set the stage for a constant flow of ideas and inspiration that will continue to propel you forward.

2 Find Your Purpose

Everyone travels for a reason. It can be as simple as finally having the time to settle in and sip an umbrella drink in a beach chair, or realizing your dream of using your skills as a volunteer. Once you've identified the *where* on your travel Wish List, spend some time with the *why*, which in turn will often lead you to the *how*. For example, you might volunteer to teach English or build schools with an organization such as Discover Corps or Road Scholar, and then spend some time traveling to explore the area.

3 Do Your Homework

Learn everything you can about your travel destinations. Research all of the options for traveling on a budget to find out which ones fit your goals, interests, and travel style.

Start with the Internet. A few simple Google searches will provide hours of online reading. Look for travel blogs that you relate to, and sign up to receive their posts. Make connections. Share your dream. When you start telling people about your retirement-travel goals, you will be surprised how many like-minded people you will meet and the information and opportunities that will come your way. Set the wheels of adventure in motion *now*.

4 Test the Waters with Mini Trips

You may not be ready to sell the house and everything in it and head out to see the world quite yet, but you can start flexing your adventure muscle with mini trips. If walking the Camino de Santiago is on your bucket list, start by exploring your city on foot. Sign up for a three-hour walking tour or create your own. Life, and your city, look very different when you slow down to 3 mph. Do you dream of traveling across Europe with just a Eurail pass and your backpack? Why not start with Amtrak, your backpack, and a quick weekend getaway a couple of hours from home.

5 Hone Your Language Skills

Many Americans assume that everyone speaks English abroad. This may be the case in big cities, but not once you step off the well-worn path. Wherever you travel, you will have a very different experience if you have at least a basic understanding of their language. The ability to say good morning and engage in a simple conversation truly enhances your "live like a local" experience. Check out the continuing-education catalog at your community college for classes in Spanish, French, German, or Japanese. Join a local language-exchange group through Meetup or your library. Generally, these groups meet weekly, and half of the conversation is in English and half is in the language you are learning. You will meet native speakers and learn about different customs and cultures while you are improving your speaking skills.

6 Take the Road Less Traveled

Going just a little bit off the beaten path can save you substantial money. I've found that if you stay in that lovely small town just outside of the big city, the prices for both food and lodging will usually drop dramatically.

{ "You can save a lot of money and have a much richer time if you live more like a local and less like a tourist." }

If you missed that gap year of travel in your 20s, here is your second chance to pack up your backpack and head out to explore the world. With retirement travel, you have the luxury of time all over again. Take as long as you like and enjoy every minute. You've earned it.

See you on the road!

LEARNING NEVER RETIRES

BY KALI LIGHTFOOT

A leader in the field of lifelong learning gives her prescription for creating a stimulating retirement.

Kali Lightfoot is executive director of the National Resource Center for Osher Lifelong Learning Institutes (OLLIs) and previously was on the management staff at Elderhostel (now known as Road Scholar). She has also taught in high school and college, and served as a wilderness ranger for the U.S. Forest Service. Kali is a graduate of Leadership Maine, and past chair of the Lifetime Education and Renewal Network of the American Society on Aging.

FEEDING THE BRAIN IN RETIREMENT

"Always read something that will make you look good if you die in the middle of it." —P. J. O'Rourke

Do you have an inquisitive nature, a curiosity about life, a passion for a special interest? There is mounting evidence that the best things you can do for yourself in retirement are:

- get plenty of exercise,
- nurture your curiosity,
- and maintain positive, strong social connections.

Lifelong-learning institutes and other adult-learning programs are a great way to do all three.

{ "Lifelong–learning institutes provide wonderful ways to meet people." }

In retirement, you'll be able to put your curiosity and passion to good use by seeking out courses in any one of the approximately 600 lifelong-learning institutes in the United States. Most are connected to college campuses, but you can also find them affiliated with public libraries, senior centers, and adult-residential communities. The two best sources of information about institutes and the locations nearest you are the Road Scholar Institute Network (roadscholar.org/n/institute-network-lifelong-learning) and the National Resource Center for Osher Lifelong Learning Institutes (osher.net).

In addition to the helpful map of Osher Institutes, the National Resource Center provides a wealth of information: links to books and blogs written by OLLI members, educational travel opportunities, videos from OLLIs, archives of the monthly national newsletter, research on lifelong learning, announcements of upcoming conferences, and materials from previous conferences. There is also a library on our Web site containing information and sample documents that are useful to leaders of lifelong-learning institutes. You will find the same kinds of information on the Road Scholar Institute Network site.

What should you expect when you embark on lifelong learning? No tests, no credits, no grades, and no homework (unless you want to do some!). Just learning for the pure joy of it, in a community of people with a passion for learning, who are generally over age 50. The institutes are a place to find courses on just about any subject you can think of. You didn't go to college as a youngster? No problem. What you have learned through living is more than enough to let you fit right in. At any institute, you will find Ph.D.'s sitting next to high-school graduates in the same class.

WHAT DO YOU GET AT A LIFELONG-LEARNING INSTITUTE?

All classes are geared to adults, and the topics cover a broad range of interests, from history and current events to literature, music, art, and beyond. Here are some sample course titles from OLLIs around the country:

- Celtic Myth and Legend
- The Lion's Roar: The Life and Turbulent Times of Winston L. S. Churchill
- One Culture: Science and the Humanities
- Books That Changed America
- Discovering Our Mother's Stories: A Course for Daughters
- Immigration to the U.S. — Voluntary and Involuntary
- History of Rhythm and Blues
- Line Dancing: A Cross-Cultural Perspective
- Beginning French
- Huckleberry Finn and Mark Twain, Two Missouri Boys Who Changed the World
- Contemporary Film
- A Modern View of Biblical Women

- Introduction to Bird Study
- The Language of Sculpture

Many institutes are managed by their members, who volunteer on boards and committees, and pitch in to lead activities or help with special events. The Osher Institutes usually employ paid staff who lead volunteers, while many of the institutes that don't have the Osher name rely solely on volunteers to manage all of the activities. In either case, there are lots of opportunities to get involved. Many of the classes are taught by members, so your teacher might be a retired professor, a community leader, or just someone with a lifelong passion for a particular topic. If you are a teacher yourself, or interested in becoming one, the students are some of the most lively and engaged you will ever teach.

Most of the institutes also offer special-interest groups for members who want to get together to hike, play mah-jongg, play music, sing, talk, or do one of a myriad of other activities.

And all of that wealth of learning and activity is available for very low membership fees. Perks of membership often include access to the university library and athletic facilities, and discounts on plays on campus. Each institute is priced differently, but expect a true bargain — sometimes as low as $25 for annual membership, plus tuition as low as $50 for an eight-week class. Classes at institutes may meet for four or more weeks, or some are just single-session lectures.

LEARNING IS SOCIAL

At the beginning of this essay, I mentioned the importance of social connections in retirement. Lifelong-learning institutes provide wonderful ways to meet people. Many who retire move to new communities, and OLLIs are great places to learn about your surroundings as well as find friends who share the same — or different — interests. The institutes are full of outgoing, active people who are curious about the world around them.

> "The institutes are full of outgoing, active people who are curious about the world around them."

Love to travel, see new places, and learn about diverse cultures? Many lifelong-learning institutes offer day trips to interesting local sites, overnight trips to the next county or the other side of the country, or trips to international destinations. All of the travel programs are designed to be learning adventures, not just tourist tromps. In addition to sightseeing, you will go behind the scenes to explore the real stories of people and places throughout history and up to the present day. Often, the trips are paired with a class beforehand at your learning institute, so you will arrive at a destination prepared to take in all that the locale has to offer.

A "NOVEL" APPROACH TO BRAIN HEALTH

Neurologists now know that each time you learn something new, your brain opens up new neural pathways. There is no conclusive research yet, but neuroscientist Paul Nussbaum (paulnussbaum.com) reports that our brains need exposure to environments that are enriched, complex, and "novel"(new); such exposure across your lifespan will lead to new brain-cell development and increased cellular connections, or "brain reserve." Indications are that this reserve may help to delay the onset of neurogenerative diseases such as Alzheimer's and related dementias.

Also, the more parts of your *physical self* that are involved in that learning, the better. Dr. Nussbaum says we need to engage in activities that are novel and complex, too, requiring more than just reading. He has written several well-regarded books on keeping your brain healthy, including *Save Your Brain* and *Your Brain Health Lifestyle,* in which he recommends focusing on learning one new activity every year, whether it's studying to play an instrument, becoming fluent in a second or third language, building a kayak, or learning to ballroom dance. Here are some additional activities recommended by Dr. Nussbaum:

- practice writing with your nondominant hand
- play a new board game
- play a new sport
- relax (stress can interfere with healthy brain development)

OPTIONS FOR LEARNING TO EXPLORE

If you are interested in more practical or hands-on learning than the courses offered at your local lifelong-learning institute, be sure to check out places in your town that might offer instruction. Here is a list of possibilities, but keep your eyes and ears open for other options as well:

- local community colleges
- adult-ed programs at high schools
- crafts centers
- art schools
- nature centers

- woodworking stores
- computer stores
- kitchen stores
- high-end grocery stores
- public libraries
- the hospital education department

Ever wanted to go to college? Not sure you are "college material"? You now have loads of options to try out a college course before actually plunking down the money to start a degree program. MOOCs (Massive Open Online Courses) are cropping up everywhere online. All you need is a computer, basic skills, and a desire to learn — and the courses are free. You will be taught through video lectures by excellent professors (often with opportunities for interactive messaging), and online discussions with your classmates. You can be as actively engaged as you want to be, taking tests and doing writing assignments, or you can just enjoy watching the course unfold in front of you. Here are a few Web sites where you can view course catalogs. The courses are fully equal to those offered at any college:

Coursera: coursera.com

Harvard Edx: extension.harvard.edu/open-learning-initiative

Stanford Open Courses: class-central.com/university/stanford

WHAT LIFELONG LEARNERS HAVE TO SAY

As the executive director of the National Resource Center at for Osher Lifelong Learning Institutes (OLLI), I've been privileged to hear from the many students over 50 years old who have taken courses and expanded their horizons. I'd like to share some of their inspiring comments with you.

"My advice to a new member of OLLI is 'Don't be merely a consumer. Join in: take classes, give classes, join committees. Exercise your creative energy in every way you can. The rewards of the WHOLE experience are life giving and life affirming.'"

—Keith Sherburne, student, teacher, and board member at OLLI at the University of Southern Maine

"We are redefining aging. I believe we are the greatest generation. When 50-to-90-year-olds network and gather together, it is truly a timeless, cross-generational experience. We are a bridge through the ages, embracing cumulative wisdom, experience, thought, and learning. This is an amazing process of enlightenment and one for celebration. I stand in awe of the whole thing, and at the same time, I feel so connected to and embraced by it all."

—Lyndee Kaput, member and volunteer, OLLI at California State University, Chico

"My favorite part of OLLI is getting to know people that I never imagined I'd have so much in common with. Take courses, study groups, trips, any kind of OLLI activity that strikes your fancy. You'll be amazed at how it will repay your effort in ways you never imagined."

—Peter Michalove, member/instructor, OLLI at the University of Illinois

ONE WOMAN'S VIEW
SUSAN'S STORY: "OLLI has turned out to be a real blessing"

Susan Levine, OLLI program assistant, member, and peer leader, OLLI at California State University, Chico, commented on her experience with the program:

> *After being retired due to cutbacks in my hours, I was sad and missing the challenge of my job as an elementary school library clerk. I felt I had contributed to the children and staff that I had served. I had taught hundreds of fifth graders to play the card game cribbage over the previous ten years, so my friend who taught French at OLLI suggested I teach cards to seniors. I had never heard of OLLI. I was then 60. I contacted the director, taught my first group, and rediscovered a passion in my life. It is so rewarding to me to be part of an educational system again. I guess it's in my blood. Even my husband, who wanted nothing to do with it, has joined in and is benefiting from the organization. He is meeting new people, which is great because he's a shy person, and after retiring he was home all the time. OLLI is a nonthreatening, positive way for him to socialize, and that's so important for emotional and mental health. OLLI has turned out to be a real blessing in both our lives."*

Retirement Plan Ahead **Action Steps**

In summary, the old saw "you can't teach an old dog new tricks" is just that, an old saw, and absolutely not true. You can learn at any age, and learning is not only fun, but good for your health and vital to a happy retirement. Through lifelong-learning institutes, you can acquire new skills, discover fascinating ideas, become engaged in your community, and meet interesting people who will become friends for life.

1 Are You in the Right Place?

Are you living in the best place to take advantage of lifelong-learning opportunities? Do you have access to libraries, adult education, colleges, lifelong-learning institutes, arts programs, and other venues for learning? If not, perhaps your retirement plans should include a move. And if you are already thinking about moving, add "opportunities for learning" to your checklist for a new community.

2 Nurture Your Curiosity

Every day brings you opportunities to learn new things. Think about who you are as a learner. Do you like to be outdoors and active? Do you enjoy lectures? Do you like meaty discussions — enjoy a good controversy? Do you like to create art or look at art? What have you always wanted to learn about but never had the opportunity (or the courage!) to try?

3 Research Your Local Lifelong-Learning Institute

If there is a lifelong-learning institute in your area, look online at their course offerings and activities. Visit their office and ask if you can sit in on several courses for a day. Check the cost and be sure to plan for that when you create your retirement budget.

4 Be Proactive!

If there isn't any lifelong-learning institute near you, find out how you can start one. The National Resource Center for OLLIs and the Road Scholar Institute Network both have start-up materials available with step-by-step instructions. Check out osher.net and roadscholar.org.

5 Teach Others

One of the best ways to stay engaged and continue learning is to teach others. What do you have a passion for that others might like to learn? Think about what you would need to learn in order to teach. Find a mentor who can help you get started.

LEARNING LATER, LIVING GREATER!

BY NANCY MERZ NORDSTROM, M.Ed.

A proponent of lifelong learning shows how it can benefit the mind, body, and spirit.

A dedicated lifelong learner, Nancy Merz Nordstrom returned to school after the unexpected death of her first husband, and at age 53, earned an M.Ed. in Adult Education. As a later-life student, she became aware of the opportunities and challenges facing older adults, and firmly believes lifelong learning is both empowering and life affirming, regardless of age.

LIVE TO LEARN

Imagine the stimulation of exploring the historical and cultural treasures in a nearby museum, or the thrill of taking part in a lively discussion about the life and works of Vincent van Gogh, or the satisfaction that comes from discovering that math isn't so hard after all. There's no doubt such experiences will spice up your life and add joy and vitality to your retirement years.

In thinking about those years, you've probably wondered what they will look like, how you can make them as satisfying as possible, and what new ideas and directions might help enhance them and provide you with a more fulfilling life.

Well, as an old Portuguese proverb says, "Live to learn and you will learn to live." This is so right. Lifelong learning is the answer.

Thanks to a vast array of opportunities available in the learning world today, older adults now have the chance to make their later years far more exciting than they ever dreamed possible. Incorporating lifelong learning into our "after-50" years means our minds will be more stimulated, our bodies more active, and our spirits more fulfilled.

FIND LIFE SATISFACTION

Lifelong learning is noncredit education for the sheer joy of discovering new thoughts, ideas, and information. It can enrich one's retirement and create new social connections. In later years, it's the perfect opportunity for people to take part in all the things they never had time for while working and/or raising a family.

To some degree, everyone is a lifelong learner. If you read a newspaper, do crossword puzzles, or read a good book, you are taking part in informal lifelong learning. What we are talking about here, however, are more deliberate ways to engage your brain and reap the numerous benefits of keeping mentally active.

One lifelong learner sums it up this way: *"We have an amazing program for self-discovery. We base everything on the belief that our capacity to learn and grow does not decrease as our years increase. In fact, through learning and the adventures we embark on, we actually embrace self-fulfillment."*

Now that is life satisfaction!

JOIN THE MIND/BODY/SPIRIT HEALTH CLUB

Lifelong learning is truly a holistic health club. Here's how it works:

Our Minds

Just like our hearts, our minds need to be nurtured. According to recent research, our brains actually respond to enriching mental activities and can even grow new connections and pathways when challenged and stimulated. That being the case, lifelong learning is definitely a health club for our minds.

Our Bodies

Along with keeping our minds alert and agile as we age, everyone knows the importance of keeping our bodies active. Lifelong-learning programs can be found at universities, colleges, and adult-education centers, and they offer many ways to incorporate activity into our daily lives. Along with more traditional courses, most programs offer a variety of fitness classes, such as swimming, aerobics, walking clubs, hiking, birding, bicycling, and yoga. Classes in spirituality, meditation, stress reduction, and outdoor programs, just to name a few, round out the exhilarating curriculum. Taking part in classes helps people stick with it, leading to even more activity — the perfect health club!

Our Spirits

Finally, lifelong learning engages our spirits. It provides the needed social interaction that is often lacking as people age. Outdoor programs, field trips, luncheons, parties, and travel far and near give mature adults the opportunity to make new friends and engage in stimulating give-and-take discussions. Life gets a little overwhelming at times. How better to get through those challenges than by sharing them with other lifelong learners?

Lifelong learning can also help us:

- achieve goals
- open doors to new thoughts and social interactions
- increase our sense of self-worth
- fulfill the human desire to discover and understand

When we are able to fulfill these basic desires, we are also setting ourselves up for that life satisfaction we all seek. A health club that takes care of our minds, our bodies, and our spirits is a club everyone will want to join.

START REAPING THE BENEFITS

Learning in our later years offers us many benefits, including:

- helping us fully exploit our natural abilities while striving to lessen our faults
- giving us the chance to immerse ourselves in the wonders of life
- providing us with a measure of how our lives should be lived to the best of our ability
- pointing out the pitfalls of life so we can avoid them in our pursuit of happiness
- teaching us to look beyond the surface and see the truth as it really is
- stimulating our natural curiosity about the world around us
- helping us increase our wisdom during our later years, and use our experiences to make the world a better place

HAVE FUN

People also become involved in lifelong-learning programs as much for the socialization as for the education. Participants find old friends and make new ones, and some have even found new spouses!

Take a look at some of the many events lifelong learners take part in:

- walking and hiking clubs
- theatre trips
- dinner clubs
- book clubs
- current-events groups
- theme festivals
- chess clubs
- bird clubs
- special-interest groups of all types

So, whether you want to continue learning to keep abreast of the latest news or the newest innovations, or because you want to continue to grow and have fun, it's all there for you in the world of lifelong learning — a world of your own making, personalized just for you, based on your own needs and desires.

DEVELOP YOUR ACTION PLAN

Today, there is a wealth of opportunities in our communities to continue learning. Here are some suggestions to help you develop your action plan:

- colleges and universities
- senior centers and adult-retirement communities
- libraries and churches
- museums and adult-education centers
- lifelong-learning programs for older adults
- community lectures
- special-interest organizations
- book clubs
- study circles
- senior theatre
- the Internet

These are just a few of the lifelong-learning opportunities that can be found in your community and online. They are meant to be a starting point on your journey of self-discovery as you seek and gain greater knowledge.

If you keep your eyes and ears open, and read notices on bulletin boards, the small print in newspapers, and local flyers in stores, libraries, and other places, you will begin to realize just how many choices and selections there are right in your own backyard to keep your mind stimulated, your body active, and your spirit alive. Searching them out is half the fun.

If you're interested in a more structured, noncredit lifelong-learning program, perhaps on a college or university campus, then check out a list of more than 400 such programs in the United States by visiting roadscholar.org/rsin.

TAKE THE LIFELONG-LEARNING QUIZ

Not sure if you're a lifelong learner? Answering these questions will help point you in the right direction. If you answer 'yes' to five or more questions, you are a lifelong learner.

1. Do you like to make things happen instead of waiting to react to situations?

2. Would you describe yourself as someone who obtained a significant portion of your knowledge outside of a formal classroom?

3. Are there always things you'd love to know more about or wish you could appreciate more deeply?

4. Do you experience positive feelings about yourself when you learn something new?

5. Can you identify certain personal life experiences as times of immense learning, even though they probably wouldn't be defined as "classes" or "courses"?

6. Are you open to new ideas and experiences?

7. Do you enjoy gaining the perspectives and wisdom of others?

8. Are you awed by the infinite nature of knowledge, and do you feel that you could never possibly know everything you want to know in life?

START LIVING GREATER BY LEARNING LATER

Every day we are given new choices and opportunities. It's the way we select them that gives our life meaning. So, if you decide lifelong learning has a place in your life, you can choose to seek out opportunities in your community to expand your knowledge and wisdom. You will find your life becoming richer, fuller, and far more satisfying.

An old Chinese proverb says, "Learning is a treasure that will follow its owner everywhere." Great treasures await you in the lifelong-learning world.

ONE WOMAN'S VIEW
BETTY'S STORY: "Lifelong learning . . . keeps my world growing."

Recently retired with my 60th birthday looming, I found myself wondering, 'what's next?' Several days later, a small announcement in our local paper caught my eye. A series of lectures on Tuesday mornings over the course of several months was being offered through a lifelong-learning program at a nearby college. Each lecture examined a different topic. Some were topics I knew a bit about; others were completely new. I gave them all a try. Now, a few months later, thanks to being exposed to people who want to keep learning, I find my knowledge of what's happening in our community greatly increased. In fact, I just signed up for a literature course on great American novels that I learned about from one of the attendees. I'm finding that lifelong learning expands my mind, energizes me, and keeps my world growing. What a gift for the curious mind."

{ "Are you open to new ideas and experiences?" }

Retirement **Plan Ahead** Action Steps

Even if your retirement years are still well in the future, here are some suggestions to help you begin thinking about incorporating lifelong learning into your life.

1 Start a Lifelong-Learning Notebook

Jot down all your thoughts and ideas, and any information you learn about programs and courses in your community. Keep it somewhere safe so you can update it regularly and refer to it as needed.

2 Create a Vision and a Strategy for Your Later Life

Map out future goals that include lifelong learning as well as other interests you'd like to pursue. Think about ways to make this happen.

3 Develop a "Want to Learn" List

Think about the subjects and topics you've always wanted to find out more about. Keep adding to this list in the coming years.

4 Visit Several Different Types of Lifelong-Learning Programs

You will be warmly welcomed.

5 Think About Your Postwork in an Upbeat Way

Write down all the positives. This will go a long way toward creating an environment conducive to successful learning and living.

THE VALUE OF VOLUNTEERING

BY SHIRLEY SAGAWA

An acclaimed pioneer of the volunteer movement in America describes how volunteering can enhance your retirement years.

Named a "Woman to Watch in the 21st Century" by *Newsweek* and one of the "Most Influential Working Mothers in America" by *Working Mother* magazine, Shirley Sagawa has been called a "founding mother of the modern service movement." Her recent book, *The American Way to Change*, describes a new role for volunteer service to help solve the nation's biggest problems. Marrying a dozen years as a consultant to nonprofits at sagawa/jospin with decades of experience in the policy arena — as an architect of AmeriCorps, on the White House staff, as counsel to the Senator Labor Committee, and as a fellow at the Center for American Progress — she offers a fresh look at the value of volunteering.

THE VALUE OF VOLUNTEERING

Did you know that volunteering makes you live longer?

Research shows that older people who volunteer at least once a week not only live longer, they are happier and healthier too, both mentally and physically, with lower rates of pain, depression, and heart disease and higher functional ability.

In thinking about those years you've probably wondered what they will look like, how you can make them as satisfying as possible, and what new ideas and directions might help enhance them and provide a more fulfilling life.

> "Older people who volunteer at least once a week not only live longer, they are happier and healthier too."

It makes sense: volunteering gets you out of the house and gives you a chance to meet and see other people, another key to a healthy, long life. Many people volunteer to learn new skills or test out a new field — a good strategy if you're looking to pursue an encore career in a helping field. Even if an encore career is not in the works, volunteering is a great way to learn and experience new things — including travel.

Volunteering can also give you a sense of purpose. Experts define purpose as the intention to accomplish something that is both meaningful to you and consequential for others. It's key to healthy development among youth. But having a sense of purpose is as important to older adults as it is to adolescents — it's not by accident that the founder of the AARP adopted the motto "To Serve, Not to Be Served." In fact, according to one study (psychosomaticmedicine.org/content/71/5/574.abstract), a person with a high purpose in life, someone who derives meaning from life's experiences and possesses a sense of intentionality and goal directedness, was more likely to live longer than a person who lacked a high purpose.

> "Volunteering is a great way to learn and experience new things."

THINKING AHEAD

While many older adults begin to look for volunteering opportunities when they retire, starting early can ensure you will have meaningful opportunities to contribute from day one.

To get started, think about causes you care about. For example, what are you passionate about?

- Do you love the theater?
- Helping poor kids?
- Transforming rundown neighborhoods?
- Saving endangered animals?

Find out what organizations work on the issues that inspire you. My book, *The American Way to Change,* offers surprising ways that volunteers can make a difference in a wide range of areas.

Begin to think about the role that volunteering might play in your retirement. The chart on the next page will help you to consider various options.

> "Starting early can ensure you will have meaningful opportunities to contribute from day one."

IF YOU'RE LOOKING FOR:	CONSIDER:
Social opportunities	Joining a club or congregation that organizes volunteer opportunities for members
A support network	Joining or starting a time bank
An encore career	Volunteering in the field you are interested in to build connections and experience
New experiences	Volunteering in a neighborhood across town or on a project in another community
A full-time opportunity	AmeriCorps or pro-bono work with an organization that can use full-time help
The chance to be around young people	Schools, youth organizations, tutoring and mentoring programs, or early-childhood-development programs
New skills	Organizations that provide training to volunteers
Cultural opportunities	Theaters, museums, and other organizations (many will offer tickets or classes to their volunteers)
Travel	Volunteer vacations or the Peace Corps
Exercise	Coaching a sports team, performing physical service outdoors, or leading others in a community exercise program, walking tour, or hike
A way to spend time with family	Intergenerational or family volunteering
Leadership positions	Board service

Armed with this information, do some research about organizations that might offer opportunities that meet your needs and interests. Building a relationship with these organizations now can pay dividends in the future. You might start attending events or meetings hosted by the organization, learn more about its work, and even try volunteering.

Other steps you can take now:

- Join a religious congregation or social club that volunteers
- Develop skills nonprofits need — for example, take a class in grant writing, learn to teach English as a Second Language, or become a skilled photographer
- Identify like-minded friends who are interested in volunteering with you
- Try out different opportunities to see what you like and what you don't
- Join or start a Time Bank (see page 149)
- Find out if your company has a volunteer program that includes retirees

THE EXPERIENCES OF VOLUNTEERS

"During my short time with Experience Corps, I've felt like my life has meaning. I have a reason for getting up in the morning, knowing that I am going to help a child. When they say, 'Miss Bell, I need some help,' or 'Miss Bell, will you help me?' it gives me a feeling that I am needed. You cannot imagine the joy that it brings me. I now have a purpose . . . knowing that there are children waiting for me."

—Delores Bell, Experience Corps member, Baltimore
(Story courtesy of Experience Corps)

"I joined the Peace Corps in 2006 at the age of 53, and found myself in a country very similar to my Eastern European–rooted childhood in suburban Cleveland, Ohio. The attention to home-cooked food, religious traditions, and the way people gathered and worked were so similar to customs I had grown up with that during most of my stay I felt like I was 11 years

old again — listening to my mom and aunts as I learned to cook family favorites, watching my dad and uncles work, and walking out the door each morning to new adventures."
—Patrice Koerper, Peace Corps, Macedonia
(Story courtesy of the Peace Corps)

"I'm a breast-cancer survivor, and I help women who've had surgery for breast cancer. I've volunteered for the Reach to Recovery program for 22 years. Reach to Recovery works because all the volunteers helping women through the trauma of breast cancer and surgery have been there themselves. Seeing the volunteers, women know they can beat this. It's critical that women see a survivor. A patient's eyes light up when I say it's been 29 years since I had my operation. . . . I guarantee anyone who volunteers will feel better emotionally, physically, and psychologically. I don't care who you are or what you do. The people I know who volunteer have smiles on their faces. The hours they give are worth more to them than any money they could ever receive."
—Katherine Pener, Reach to Recovery volunteer, Miami Beach (Story courtesy of Network for Good)

OPTIONS FOR VOLUNTEERING IN RETIREMENT

One-time "episodic" volunteer projects: If you can't make a long-term commitment, there are many short-term or "done in a day" opportunities, from building a playground to staffing a charity 10K.

Long-term engagement: If you can commit a few hours a week for a few months or longer, look for organizations that need your help on an ongoing basis. They may offer training and other benefits to regular volunteers. Schools, libraries, literacy programs, mentoring organizations, thrift shops, and museums often offer these kinds of opportunities.

Pro-bono work: Whether you're an accountant, a graphic designer, a chef, or a computer specialist, your professional skills could be put to use at nonprofits, schools, and other community organizations.

Volunteer vacations: Combine your love of travel with the chance to make a difference through a volunteer vacation. Even better, the travel costs could be tax deductible.

Board service: Every nonprofit has a volunteer board that governs the organization and helps in other ways. Board service is a great way to be a leader without the day-to-day pressures of running an organization. Boards may meet once a month or a few times a year.

Fund-raising: Almost every nonprofit organization needs help raising money. Helping to plan a fund-raising event is a great way to meet people if you love entertaining. Or if you'd rather keep your writing skills sharp, offer to draft a grant proposal to a foundation.

Peace Corps service: If you can spend a year overseas, the Peace Corps offers the chance to become immersed in another culture by using your skills to help the people of developing nations and emerging democracies.

National service: AmeriCorps is the domestic version of the Peace Corps. By serving full-time or half-time, you not only gain deep experience and connections in a community, you may also earn a modest living allowance and an education award you can use to take college classes. You can also transfer the award to your children or grandchildren.

Social entrepreneurship: Older adults are starting their own programs in record numbers.

Think About Time Banks

Time banks enable neighbors to earn an hour of help for each hour of volunteer service they provide.

Imagine a community in which any person in need might request help, and any person able to contribute could respond — and earn the right to assistance they might need in the future. An hour of babysitting by a retired person might be repaid by an hour of driving by a young adult. Or an hour of errands for a homebound older adult might be repaid by an hour of reading to a child. Time banks make these exchanges possible across a community of dozens or hundreds of participants who earn time by contributing to those who ask and spend the credits they earn by requesting services from others.

It's easy to start or join a time bank — timebanks.org will tell you how.

• RESOURCES •

Organizations that can connect you to volunteer opportunities:

- Hands On Action Centers
- United Way affiliates
- Mayor's office (check to see if your mayor has a service plan at CitiesofService.org)
- AARP
- Taproot Foundation
- RSVP (The Retired and Senior Volunteer Program)

Want to build a house in Costa Rica or teach English to orphans in Africa? Find volunteer vacations at:

- PodVolunteering.org

- Habitat.org
- Projects-Abroad.org
- GVIUSA.com (Global Vision International)
- GlobeAware.org
- SierraClub.org
- WorldTeach.org
- VAOPS.com (Volunteer Abroad)
- The International Volunteer Programs Association, volunteerinternational.org, which offers information about how to choose a volunteer-vacation operator

Excellent Web sites to find volunteer opportunities:

- AllforGood.org
- CreatetheGood.org
- VolunteerMatch.org
- Idealist.org
- GreatNonprofits.org
- Serve.gov
- MyAmeriCorps.gov

Great organizations to volunteer for — these national organizations may have affiliates in your community:

- Citizen Schools
- Habitat for Humanity
- Reading Partners
- Keep America Beautiful
- Share Our Strength
- Experience Corps
- KaBOOM!

- College Summit
- Junior Achievement
- Big Brothers Big Sisters
- American Cancer Society
- The American Red Cross
- LIFT Communities
- Girls on the Run

{ "Look for organizations that need your help on an ongoing basis." }

Retirement Plan Ahead **Action Steps**

1 Do Research

Think about causes you care about and research organizations that work on those issues (using some of the online search tools for volunteering).

2 Take Inventory

Inventory organizations you're already involved with to see if they offer volunteer opportunities.

3 Think About Skill Sets

Make a list of the skills you might bring to an organization — or start to develop skills that you would like to contribute in retirement.

4 Get Field Experience

Volunteer at a variety of different organizations to determine what you enjoy doing.

5 Ask Friends and Family to Join You

Recruit friends and family members who might enjoy volunteering with you.

START NOW – PLANNING FOR RETIREMENT BEGINS TODAY!

BY DAWN ANGELO

A highly regarded volunteer-advocate reveals how to prepare now for a fulfilling retirement.

Dawn Angelo is the Regional CEO of the American Red Cross for Western Washington. She has worked for two other national nonprofit organizations: Catholic Charities Minneapolis/St. Paul, an organization that engaged over 11,000 volunteers annually, and Volunteers of America Minnesota, which sponsored a wide range of volunteer programs, including the Retired and Senior Volunteer Program (RSVP) and Experience Corps.

MY INSPIRATIONS

In my career working in nonprofit organizations, I have met many people who described having role models or experiencing life-changing events that motivated them to volunteer. I had both. My parents were active volunteers in our small-town church and the community. My father was involved with politics, my mother in social services. Both were role models who taught me the value of helping others.

The life-changing event that inspired me occurred when I was a senior in college, during a return flight from Jerusalem,

Israel. I had just finished touring 15 different countries, where I had witnessed extreme poverty, political societies that limited individual expression, and places of historical significance decaying from neglect. Reflecting on my good fortune, I made this simple entry in my journal: "I want to volunteer. I want to give back when I get home."

> "[My parents] were role models who taught me the value of helping others."

PLANNING FOR RETIREMENT

For the past 16 years, I've had the opportunity to not only volunteer, but to work in a professional role managing volunteers. My career path has led from small, grassroots organizations to large, international non-governmental organizations (NGOs). I've worked with a wide variety of volunteers, spanning in age from 4 to 104 (yes, 104), but the average age for most of them was between 55 and 70. Often, these individuals were retired and delighted to be giving back to their communities.

As I look ahead to my own retirement (which I do not define as "not working"), I know I will tap into lessons I've learned from volunteers I've worked with over the years. Many of them had retirement goals that were transformed by the reality of their own current-day situations. But as they adjusted to situations dictated by financial and familial circumstances, they created new dreams for themselves that gave their lives a sense of purpose and fulfillment.

Most often, people's initial retirement plans seem to center predominately on saving money. Think of how many times you've seen an advertisement promoting the importance of planning for retirement. The focus is almost exclusively on personal finance. What I find interesting is how little emphasis is placed on all other aspects of retirement, such as the need for social connections. Imagine how much better our retirement years would be if we shifted that focus to replicate the networks we develop in our day-to-day work lives, as we spend time with individuals around the watercooler or doing work together. In retirement, we could find meaningful new ways to build social contacts and be productive — by volunteering and giving back to the community.

VOLUNTEERING

My father in-law, a prominent lawyer from California, recently shared that one of the things he misses most since retiring is spending time with colleagues. The daily routine associated with "the freedom to do whatever we want to do, whenever we want to do it" can eventually become tedious. We long for a routine that keeps us mindful of time, exposed to current events, and mentally stimulated. While some individuals are able to make the transition well, others flounder.

> "'The freedom to do whatever we want to do, whenever we want to do it' can eventually become tedious."

Volunteer service can provide meaningful opportunities that help us transition from paid, 40 hour–week work schedules to unpaid, flexible hours of work. There are so many different volunteer opportunities available. Maybe you want to teach children how to read or be a mentor in other areas. You may have an interest in serving meals at a soup kitchen or assisting those who have become homeless as a result of a disaster. Or you might want to help a young entrepreneur start a new business or offer your organizational skills to a small nonprofit organization. The opportunities are endless!

The key to all of this is getting started. Statistics show that if you haven't volunteered prior to retirement, you are unlikely to begin volunteering during your retirement years. So where should you begin?

Getting started

- **Create lists:** Identify skills and strengths that you want to offer, as well as any new skills that you want to learn. Think about the causes that interest you or the type of work you would like to do and who you would like to work with.

- **Location:** Consider where you want to volunteer. You may prefer to look for opportunities in your neighborhood, or if you're more adventurous, you might want to travel internationally.

- **Availability:** Determine how much time you have to volunteer, and be honest with yourself about your own availability. Do you have frequent business trips that take you out of town or other obligations that could impact a regular volunteer commitment?

Where to begin

- **Nonprofit organizations:** There are many organizations that promote volunteer opportunities, but consistently you will find the United Way or a local volunteer center is a great resource.

- **Personal network:** Ask your family, friends, and colleagues where they volunteer. Their service might inspire you to join them!

- **Workplace:** Most companies sponsor organized volunteer opportunities, and many even pay while you are taking time to volunteer. If your company does not do this, think about organizing a group of coworkers and sharing highlights with the Human Resource department to see if they might consider circulating news of this volunteer activity more broadly.

- **Place of worship:** No matter what your faith or spiritual belief, whether you belong to a church, synagogue, or mosque, you can often find volunteer opportunities promoted there.

- **Social media:** The Internet and other social media tools such as Facebook, Twitter, and blogs can help create a path to venues for volunteering. Search words that reflect your interests and see where they lead you!

> "Ask your family, friends, and colleagues where they volunteer."

What to expect

Screening: Be prepared to complete a volunteer application, have a background check, and provide references that can speak to your experience. Professional organizations have the same requirements as your employer. It's critical for them to know who they're taking on, especially when you consider that their volunteers are serving such populations as vulnerable youth or the elderly.

Patience: Some organizations don't have the depth or capacity to process volunteer inquiries quickly. It's not a sign indicating their lack of interest, but in small nonprofit organizations they often lack a paid volunteer manager or Human Resources staff and are dependent on just a few people to handle all the day-to-day operations, including volunteers. Negotiate arrangements that are mutually beneficial.

Commitment: If you've made it through the volunteer screening process and have been placed in a new volunteer role — congratulations! It's important to follow through on the commitment you made at the start. It's understandable that your ability to volunteer may change due to life circumstances. Just be honest with the organization where you are volunteering. They would much rather hear that your availability has changed than not hear anything at all.

· RESOURCES ·

There are many different resources that can offer you guidance as you get started. Here are a few that I recommend:

- Idealist (idealist.org)
- Points of Light (pointsoflight.org)
- Peace Corps (peacecorps.gov)
- VolunteerMatch (volunteermatch.org)
- Corporation for National and Community Service (nationalservice.gov)
- Global Volunteer Network (globalvolunteernetwork.org)

ONE WOMAN'S VIEW
KIM'S STORY: The nontraditional path to volunteering

So what happens if you make the list, check resources, and don't find the volunteer opportunity you are looking for? Is it possible to create your own volunteer work? Yes!

Kim Box was 49 years old when she decided to end her 29-year career at Hewlett-Packard. As a senior executive, she had responsibility for leading large-scale, global transformations. As she approached 50 and began to contemplate retirement, she wondered what other contributions she could make and what might bring her a new sense of fulfillment.

The leap was significant and scary, but as Kim often describes, "It was more rewarding than I ever anticipated." She began by sharing her expertise in the nonprofit sector through a variety of roles, including chairing the board of traditional nonprofit organizations like the American Red Cross and smaller grassroots organizations. However, based on her experience at HP, she found herself attracted to socially minded, for-profit enterprises.

Wijit Inc., an innovative company producing a unique driving and braking mechanism for wheelchairs, was looking for advisers with business acumen to help with strategic planning. Kim was inspired by the founder, who shared that Wijit could offer new freedom of movement to those who are wheelchair bound. She was hooked and immediately began offering guidance in developing their business plan.

It's been four years since her retirement from HP, and during that time, Kim has developed a long list of accomplishments, including:

- founder and president of the social enterprise company ParentPathway.com
- founder and executive director of Pathway to Prevention, where she led the production of the Emmy Award–winning film *Collision Course – Teen Addiction Epidemic*
- senior fellow and board member of the American Leadership Forum – Mountain Valley Chapter
- author of *Woven Leadership: The Power of Diversity to Transform Your Organization for Success*
- TedX Sacramento speaker, "Technology for Social Good"

Kim leveraged her extensive network and sense of adventure to find meaningful volunteer work.

Retirement Plan Ahead Action Steps

1 Identify What's Important

Consider the new experiences you are seeking or skills you want to learn. Write them down on a piece of paper and identify different themes that emerge.

2 Research Volunteer Opportunities

Use the same list and begin your search on the Internet. Engage coworkers, family, and friends and ask if they have any recommendations.

3 Explore Different Organizations and Opportunities

Meet with staff and/or volunteers in areas that interest you, whether traditional, social enterprise, or grassroots. You are bound to find your niche!

4 Begin the Process

Fill out any necessary volunteer application materials. Try a variety of volunteer roles.

5 Evaluate Your Decision

What may seem like the perfect fit at the start may feel different in just a few weeks or months. Set aside time to reevaluate your choice(s).

Today, we often find ourselves challenged to find balance amidst our busy work schedules, spending time with family and friends, and managing other commitments. You may wonder how you could possibly add one more activity, but keep this in mind: by making volunteering a priority, you will get far more in return than you give. Every volunteer I have ever met always reflects on how they learned something new, established friendships, and gained greater appreciation for their own abundance. I believe it will only add to your well-being and extend your retirement years.

> "By making volunteering a priority, you will get far more in return than you give."

CAREGIVING AND THE NEXT SEASON OF YOUR LIFE

BY PAULA SOLOMON, MSSS

A noted coach and family caregiver illuminates how to find personal well-being while helping others.

Paula Solomon is a life-transition coach, psychotherapist, and presenter whose passion is empowering women to create better options for themselves after midlife. She's been an eldercare and finances specialist, a consultant, and a workshop presenter at a major Boston employee-assistance program. She was also a family caregiver for more than a decade. Her work integrates knowledge of adult development, positive psychology, motivational research, and creativity. She empowers clients to design a future that reflects their passions and talents. In the book *Live Smart After 50!,* Paula wrote about practical planning to prepare for caregiving. Her Web site is TheSeasonsofYourLife.com.

BECOMING A CAREGIVER

What's *your* dream for the second half of life? Are you, like the many boomers approaching retirement age, beginning to plan with intention and think big? Is your goal to make longtime dreams happen, reconnect passionately with interests that you put aside earlier in life, or give back to others in a meaningful way? Unfortunately, these dreams rarely include thinking about how the health issues of our loved ones might impact our vision or plans. Many of us secretly hope we will not have to become caregivers, but the odds are against us.

As Rosalynn Carter said, "There are only four kinds of people in the world: those who have been caregivers, those who currently are caregivers, those who will be caregivers, and those who will need caregivers."

> "According to the U.S. Department of Health, one in four people is a caregiver for a family member or friend."

You may suddenly become a caregiver when a health crisis comes without warning, or caregiving may sneak up with incremental changes so that you don't realize how much you're doing for someone. At first, it is not hard to do a few extras, until one day you realize it is a big part of your day-to-day life. Caregiving can be full- or part-time; local or long distance; for a partner, a parent, a sibling, a disabled child, an extended family member, or a friend. However it happens, it often seems to take people by surprise that their life has changed so dramatically. It often feels like your life has been hijacked, no matter how much you care about the person you are helping.

It's natural to avoid thinking about difficulties that feel overwhelming. This leads many to put caregiving anxieties on a high shelf in the back of our mental closet. We try not to look there too often — until it becomes the reality of our lives that we can no longer avoid. Your time as a caregiver will undoubtedly be stressful; a loved one's health is declining, and both of you are dealing with continuing losses of abilities, dreams and opportunities, and eventually life. But, with meaningful conversations, advanced planning, and some strategies for self-care, we can be better prepared for the uncertainties of the caregiving journey, and make the most of the time we have with our loved one.

> "According to The National Alliance for Caregiving and the AARP, the majority of caregivers are women, and their average age is 48. One-third of them care for two or more people."

COMMUNICATION IS KEY

There is a common desire for autonomy, especially as we age. By engaging loved ones in making decisions jointly, to the degree they are able to do so, we empower them to have more say in their future. At its best, the caregiving relationship is a collaboration that takes into account the needs and abilities of *both* partners; it should address both the desires of the person needing care and the concerns of the caregiver. In the "Conversation Project," former *Boston Globe* columnist Ellen Goodman encourages families and friends to have advance discussions about end-of-life care. It is also crucial to have discussions about how to accommodate lifestyle changes necessitated by declining health before end-of-life concerns arise.

In addition to all of the practical details that need to be considered, caregiving requires good communication and a shared basic framework for how increasing needs will be met. This discussion is not easy; it requires acknowledging a future we don't want to see. To prepare for this talk, think about:

- Who might need your care? How comfortable is that relationship?

- Can you have an honest discussion about his or her wishes and how those wishes might be met?

- Have you prepared necessary financial and legal documents and discussed the financial issues for both the person needing care and your own lifestyle?

- Are you able to acknowledge possible limitations in your ability to meet some of his or her expectations/needs, and discuss what some alternative means to do that might be?

- How will you deal with differences in expectations or opinions about care alternatives and choices?

Wisdom from Caregivers

"I thought of myself as a good project manager and a whiz at dealing with bureaucracy. But figuring out all that was required (to help my mother) defeated me at first. I'd advise others to start everything earlier than you think you need to. It's all harder if it feels urgent." —Annie

"I feared I would fail in some way. I was surprised that I was able to do it — that I could be relied on — despite hellish moments of sickness, fatigue, and anger." —Jackie

---

CAREGIVING AND SELF-CARE

Caregiving impacts every aspect of life, for both the caregiver and the care recipient. Caring for someone with declining health can feel like painfully pulling off a large Band-Aid very slowly as health declines and needs increase. This ends when the loved one dies, an even bigger loss.

It is a delicate balance to do your best for your loved one while maintaining your own well-being. It's crucial to avoid mortgaging your future for your loved one's present. Your life will likely go on when your caregiving role is over, and you will need time to heal from your loss without worrying about your own finances and health.

An important lesson my mother taught me during the time I helped care for her was that being attentive to my own health needs and emotional well-being was not selfish, but a gift to her. She would occasionally say, "I want you to take care of yourself, both because I love you, and because I need you to be well. If something happened to you, I would be in serious trouble." She would courageously encourage me to go on vacations, or skip visiting her if she thought I sounded tired or appeared stressed. Whether or not your loved one can say it so clearly, know that maintaining your health and well-being is a way to be there for him or her for the long run.

Caregivers: Learning from Experience

"I concentrated solely on my husband's needs for years before I realized I'd gone three years without a full night's sleep. Only after I was taken to the hospital by ambulance was I able to acknowledge I couldn't do it all anymore. Although no one would care for him as I did, I accepted that he needed more care than I could provide, and by visiting him often at the nursing home I'd keep him in my life." —Gail

"Maintaining my husband's quality of life was my priority, so I put other interests on a back burner until my caregiving role ended. Then it occurred to me that he just might outlive me! So I did my best to fit some of the activities that gave me pleasure and joy into my life, rather than just putting them off." —Nancy

---

SELF-CARE STRATEGIES

☐ *Take care of your physical self with rest, healthy eating, exercise, medical care, and whatever stress-management practice works for you.*

☐ *Creatively find ways to stay engaged with your own passions and interests — cultivate activities that enable you to replenish your emotional energy.*

☐ *Keep up with social connections.*

☐ *Encourage and enable your loved ones to do as much as they can for themselves. They'll feel like less of a burden, and more engaged.*

☐ *Learn to prioritize by triaging all that you feel needs to be done, and letting go of the less important "to-dos." Learn to say "no" in a loving, caring way.*

☐ *Ask family and friends for help that corresponds with their talents, abilities, and geography. But be aware that caregiving responsibilities are rarely divided fairly among family members.*

☐ *Consider paid/volunteer help for respite.*

☐ *Have people you can talk to about the stresses of caregiving, such as a support group, a friend, or an individual coach or therapist.*

Wisdom from Caregivers

"Share what you're doing with friends, ask for help when you need it, and above all, have a 'go-to' person that is ready with a shoulder for you to cry on." —Mary Ellen

"If you don't think you're doing enough or that you're not doing things right, ask someone, because chances are that what feels like total inadequacy to you looks like heroic fortitude to the folks on the outside." —Annie

CAREGIVER'S LESSONS

Many caregivers are surprised to see in retrospect that the experience had a "silver lining" or an important life lesson to teach them. My mother's need to move closer to me as her health declined created an opportunity for us to spend more time together and helped us get to know each other as adults. I treasure those years together. They wouldn't have happened if it were not for the intimacy of caregiving.

- In the flurry of all the to-dos, don't forget the importance of just enjoying shared time and experiences with your loved one.
- Find ways to engage with your loved one that focus on his or her continuing abilities, rather than the disabilities.
- Use this opportunity to learn some family history, stories, or skills from your loved one. Time together may be limited, so do it now!

My mother dealt with her declining abilities with the maxim "we have no control over the cards we are dealt in life, but we *can* choose how we will play our hand." May you find ways to "play your hand well" and make this part of your life journey meaningful.

Retirement Plan Ahead **Action Steps**

1 Begin the Conversation Now

Talk with your loved one about his or her desires, and the practical questions that a possible need for future assistance may trigger. Jointly plan for what might be needed, and explore possible solutions. It's not an easy discussion, but it's the best way for people to have some control of their future care, and for caregivers to know that they are taking their loved one's preferences into account.

2 Promise Only What You Can Deliver

Avoid making blanket promises about what you will do for your loved one (e.g., that you will never put him or her into a nursing home). It's impossible to know what lies ahead, and what will be required to fulfill such a promise. You might instead promise "to do your best to meet this request," acknowledging that circumstances might not make that possible.

3 Have Important Information Readily Accessible

Gather together all essential information, including legal and health documents (such as a medical proxy and HIPAA release). Hospitals and doctors cannot legally share health information without this release. Create a list of important names and phone numbers, including your loved one's health-care providers, local hospitals, ambulance services, health-insurance information, and neighbors' phone numbers. This will be invaluable in case of emergency.

4 Engage a Local Support Team in the Plan

Try to engage extended family members. In addition, if you do not live nearby your loved one, organize a support team (friends, neighbors, and professional-care managers) that is local to your loved one to help out with the many tasks needed when a health crisis arises. Even if you are nearby, having others whom you can call on to share the responsibilities will substantially ease the stress.

5 Do Advance Research

Learn about the course of illnesses that your loved one may currently have, or that may run in your family. The need for higher levels of care can happen suddenly and unexpectedly. Researching the quality of facilities (such as rehabs, assisted-living facilities, and nursing homes) and knowing your loved one's preferences will increase the chance of providing the best care for him or her; this research is difficult to do in the middle of a crisis.

EXERCISE NOW FOR A HEALTHY RETIREMENT

BY ELIZABETH O'BRIEN

A respected journalist specializing in retirement issues recommends getting an exercise regimen in place for a healthy retirement.

Elizabeth O'Brien writes the "Retire Well" column for the *Wall Street Journal*'s MarketWatch.com, covering the intersection of health and wealth in retirement planning. She earned a B.A. in comparative literature from Brown University and an M.S. in journalism from Columbia University. Elizabeth lives with her husband and two young sons in Brooklyn, New York, where she tries to turn every playground visit into a workout.

"LET'S GET PHYSICAL"

What's on your bucket list for retirement? Whether you're planning to hike through Tuscany, volunteer at a soup kitchen, or play with your grandkids, it will require energy to accomplish your goals. And those who have been sedentary until they stop working won't be able to magically summon that energy on their first day of freedom. It's important to lay the groundwork for an active and healthy retirement decades in advance, through regular physical exercise.

If this sounds basic, that's because it is. Yet so many women don't establish a reservoir of stamina that they can tap into during their retirement years. Busy with family, jobs, and community, they neglect caring for themselves. So when their time finally comes, they don't have the energy to take full advantage of it.

"I see so many moms watching life from the sidelines, and it gets harder and harder to jump back in," says Denise Druce, a certified personal trainer in Salt Lake City, Utah. The key is to establish a fitness program for yourself now so that you're in shape to do all the things you want to do in retirement.

> "Lay the groundwork for an active and healthy retirement decades in advance."

About 35 percent of adults age 65 and up were obese between 2007 and 2010, according to the Centers for Disease Control and Prevention. It goes almost without saying that these folks won't enjoy as active a retirement as people who keep the pounds off. But the benefits of maintaining a healthy weight extend beyond the ability to enjoy regular swing dancing. Excess weight causes or contributes to many health problems that can worsen your quality of life.

Health problems caused or exacerbated by obesity:

- ▶ diabetes
- ▶ high blood pressure
- ▶ heart disease
- ▶ stroke
- ▶ joint pain

THE SHAPE OF THINGS TO COME

Exercise isn't just for those hoping to lose weight. It's about keeping in shape — for the present and the future. Svelte but sedentary people will lose muscle mass and aerobic capacity much more quickly than their more active peers, and that will come back to haunt them when it's time to take that hiking tour of Tuscany.

Think of it this way: in preparing for retirement, you wouldn't neglect to contribute to your 401(k), would you? Well, you need to make regular deposits into your energy bank, just as you would into your retirement account.

And while it may seem like everyone has an aunt who lived to be 97 despite a lifetime of smoking, red meat, and inactivity, you can't count on being one of those genetic lottery winners. "Those people who are protected despite their lousy lifestyle, they're the minority," says Dr. Gary Small, director of the UCLA Longevity Center and author of the book *The Alzheimer's Prevention Program.*

> "Higher fitness levels in midlife seem to be associated with lower risks of developing dementia later in life."

Indeed, the benefits of regular exercise will extend beyond your bucket-list years into the later years of your retirement, when you slow down. (Not that you should stop completely — everyone at any age can benefit from some physical activity tailored to his or her ability level.) And physical health can impact brain health. A 2013 study published in the *Annals of Internal Medicine* found that higher fitness levels in midlife seem to be associated with lower risks of developing dementia later in life.

"MOTION IS LOTION"

Science hasn't yet found a cure for Alzheimer's disease, the most common form of dementia. The goal, Dr. Small says, is to prevent the onset of Alzheimer's dementia for as long as possible. That's the stage of the disease where daily functioning becomes impaired. (Brain scans often show evidence of Alzheimer's before symptoms appear.) And according to Dr. Small, when it comes to prevention, the benefits of physical exercise are supported by research.

Dementia may be the most feared condition of older age, but exercise can help with day-to-day functioning as well. Regular physical activity strengthens muscles and improves balance, helping to prevent falls. And exercise can also help ease the joint pain of arthritis. As Denise Druce likes to tell her clients, "Motion is lotion."

If you're still not convinced, consider this: research suggests regular physical activity in midlife and beyond could mean the difference between living independently in old age and living in a care facility. Dr. Edward Schneider, professor of gerontology and medicine at the University of Southern California, saw evidence of this in his own family. His grandmother lived an active life, and at age 89, she was still spry and healthy enough to volunteer in a nursing home. Dr. Schneider's mother lived a more sedentary life, and by the time she was age 89 herself, she was a resident of a nursing home. This wasn't mere happenstance, he says; regular physical activity contributed to his grandmother's later-life independence.

MAKE A PLAN

An entrepreneur doesn't start a business — and expect to succeed — without a business plan. In the same way, if you expect to have a successful retirement, you need to create a "fitness plan." Here are some exercise recommendations for adults, from the Centers for Disease Control and Prevention:

- At least two hours and 30 minutes of moderate-intensity aerobic activity per week, such as brisk walking. (Research supports the benefits of exercise in increments as short as ten minutes. So squeeze in a walk at lunch, take the steps whenever you can, and park in the farthest spot from the store. It all adds up.)

- If you prefer a vigorous-intensity aerobic workout, you can get the same benefits from one hour and 15 minutes of an activity like jogging as you do from two and a half hours of brisk walking.

- Muscle-strengthening activities two or more two days a week that work all the major muscle groups: legs, hips, back, abdomen, chest, shoulders, and arms. Some experts recommend adding balance training to the mix. Personal trainer Druce says that this could simply involve standing on one foot when you brush your teeth in the morning, and on the other when you brush at night.

SWEAT IT!

Denise Druce also recommends that women do their age in push-ups every day. That's real push-ups — on your toes, not your knees. It doesn't have to be all at once. Druce, a fit and fabulous 50, squeezes in five sets of ten push-ups a day. The goal increases as you get older, and that's the point. Druce says that with increasing years, women need more resistance training and less cardio. And push-ups engage the whole body, working not just the arms but the core and the legs as well.

> { "Women [should] do their age in push-ups every day." }

It's fine if you start this regimen without being able to do a single push-up, Druce adds. Gradually build up your strength by supporting your weight on your toes for as long as you can — in other words, get into the push-up position but don't dip down. If you keep at it, you'll be surprised at how quickly you improve.

Beyond the physical gains, a regular push-up routine is a major confidence booster. "The best benefit for women of doing push-ups on their toes is self-esteem," Druce says. What better way to head into retirement, believing you can conquer anything?

As with many other endeavors, it's important not to let the perfect get in the way of the good when it comes to exercise. If you enjoy following the latest exercise research and want to craft a workout in accordance with it, by all means do so. But if you get anxious thinking you need to design the perfect program, don't sweat those details. Just sweat. Your 80-year-old self will thank you.

> { "It's important not to let the perfect get in the way of the good when it comes to exercise." }

ONE WOMAN'S VIEW
STACEY'S STORY: "Take care of yourself"

> I'm a gerontologist — I understand that exercise can improve quality of life in retirement. But seven years ago, at age 45, I was diagnosed with osteoporosis. There's a history of early menopause in my family, so I had a baseline bone-density test earlier than most women. Still, I was in shock with the diagnosis. I was young, thin, in excellent health. I walked and ran for exercise and never thought about osteoporosis — that was for old ladies. The doctor said to me that she was going to prescribe Fosamax for me. I decided I wouldn't take the drug. Instead, I would take a year and do weight training.

"I have a lot of girlfriends, and everyone's into yoga. Before my diagnosis, I didn't appreciate how important weight-bearing exercise was for women in their 40s and 50s. That's not yoga. Thanks to my weight training, I have reversed my bone loss and grown a quarter-inch. I exercise four to six days a week for about 45 minutes. I stretch, then walk briskly on the treadmill for 30 minutes at an incline. And I do weights. It's my prescription drug. I must do it.

"At the time of my diagnosis, I was working in the aging field at the Council for Jewish Elderly (now CJE Senior Life) in Chicago. We got a grant to do osteoporosis screenings in the community. We'd take our ultrasound machine to senior centers, libraries, and clothing stores. I became the poster child for the value of screenings."

Stacey plans to make the most of her retirement years by exercising on a regular basis now. "As women get older, you can really tell who doesn't exercise. They age so fast. They have trouble getting up. They complain about their back. If you're active and you take care of yourself, you look younger. As a good OB/GYN told me, you don't have to get matronly if you don't want to."

Retirement Plan Ahead Action Steps

1 Find an Activity You Like

For it to be sustainable, exercise has to be *fun*. If you don't like gyms, stay out of the gym. Buy a dance DVD and boogie down at home, or record your favorite shows and watch them on the treadmill. Walk briskly around the mall or take classes at your local community center.

2 Engage a Professional

If you do choose the gym route and want to start working out with weights and other equipment, consider scheduling a session with a personal trainer first. She can teach you the proper technique and help you prevent injuries.

3 Engage a Buddy

Some people prefer working out solo, but many find that it helps to have a friend to keep them accountable — and it adds a fun social factor to their workout, too.

4 Work Up to Your Goal

If you've been sedentary, don't feel like you have to start with the full amount of recommended exercise. Even one day of activity a week is a start. You'll begin to like the way you feel and want to continue.

5 Celebrate Your Success

Once you're sticking to your routine and feeling great, treat yourself. Maybe it's a dress that shows off the new tone in your arms, a spa massage, or dinner with friends. Anything that rewards you and motivates you to keep at it will do the trick.

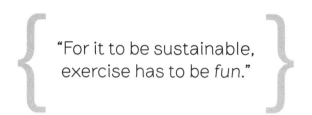

"For it to be sustainable, exercise has to be *fun*."

CREATING A CULTURE OF MOVEMENT — A SANE APPROACH TO GOOD HEALTH

BY MOIRA LANIER

A popular fitness expert makes a strong case for taking action now to prepare for an active retirement.

Moira Lanier is the founder, president, chief motivator, and head trainer of Greatest Age Fitness, Inc., a unique physical-training center for people over the age of 50 or those who want to have a head start on getting in shape for their later years. Her philosophy is to provide age-appropriate instruction, coaching, and support in a setting where people treat their bodies mindfully and respectfully in the face of aging. Moira's center is located in West Newton, Massachusetts. She is also a contributing author to *Live Smart After 50! The Experts' Guide to Life Planning for Uncertain Times* and a member of the Life Planning Network.

HOW ARE WE DOING?

We are different than our parent's generation — as boomers, we seek more dynamic, innovative careers and a more exciting, purposeful retirement. But in some important ways, we are not as healthy as our parents were when they were our age. Let's take a look at Rebecca.

ONE WOMAN'S VIEW
REBECCA'S STORY: "How do I get and stay healthy?"

Forty-nine-year-old Rebecca was profoundly perplexed. She saw pain, dysfunction, and decline all around her. She saw it, as one might expect, in people her mother's age and older who were facing their retirement years. But, to her chagrin, she felt that she was also seeing those same problems in her own life.

Dubious, but determined to take action, Rebecca joined a gym where she saw people on treadmills, plodding along with mouths agape in zombie-like trances. There were others there too, grunting and contorting, straining and jerking, lifting dumbbells that were too big for any reasonable person to lift.

After several weeks of serious workout sessions, she found herself in Ripped Torn's Physical Therapy Clinic with an inflamed triceps tendon and a hairline fracture in her foot. Rebecca soberly realized that this approach might not lead her to good health and independence as she got older.

Undeterred, she read all the popular magazines at the grocery checkout and learned how to lose 20 pounds in four weeks and still eat all of her favorite foods. All she had to do was cut back a little and engage in concurrent bouts of diuretic consumption and periodic bowel cleansings with the help of a new seaweed concoction. And she did.

A month later, recovering in the Weak Back Convalescence Home from dehydration and exhaustion, hooked up to a glucose drip, she understood that this was another path that would not lead to good health and independence as she got older.

As she pulled herself together, her brain clearer than before, Rebecca realized the folly of her misguided efforts. But if intense workouts and cleansings weren't the answers, what was she supposed to do? *"How do I to get and stay healthy?"* she asked.

ARE BABY BOOMERS REALLY AHEAD OF THE GAME HEALTHWISE?

Of course, Rebecca is a fictitious character. This parody, however, speaks to the uncertainty and confusion felt by many women as they enter middle age. What's the truth? Who does one listen to? Where does one find the answers? What's coming next and how does one prepare?

Ironically, U.S. baby boomers are often portrayed as vibrant and living the good life, with extra "bonus" years gained from a longer life expectancy. They're depicted as fulfilled, happy, and engaged.

The more than 100 million Americans who are over the age of 50 may proudly think of themselves as ahead of the game in comparison to the previous generation, when it comes to good health and quality of life. But, in reality, the evidence doesn't support that fantasy. They may be living longer, but quality of life, in terms of health and independence, is in decline and predicted to continue getting worse in the future.

In fact, U.S. baby boomers are fatter, more physically deconditioned, and suffering a higher incidence of so-called "diseases of aging" than the previous generation at the same age, according to a study in *JAMA Internal Medicine,* released in February 2013[1]. Results of the study suggest that the previous generation reported better self-assessed health status, less obesity, and more daily activity than today's U.S. baby-boomer generation. Just look at the findings on page 187.

---

[1] *JAMA Internal Medicine.* Published online February 4, 2013. doi: 10.1001/jamaintern-med.2013.2006. media.jamanetwork.com/news-item/overall-health-status-of-baby-boomers-appears-lower-than-previous-generation/

OVERALL HEALTH STATUS OF BABY BOOMERS APPEARS LOWER THAN PREVIOUS GENERATION[1]		
JAMA Internal Medicine, February 4, 2013. This study, led by Dana E. King., M.D., M.S., of the West Virginia University School of Medicine, Morgantown, analyzed data from the National Health and Nutrition Examination Surveys. The average age of the participants in the study was 54 years of age.		
SURVEY PERIODS	**BABY BOOMERS 2007-2010**	**PREVIOUS GENERATION 1988-1994**
Rated Overall Health Status as Excellent:	13.2%	32%
Occurrence of Obesity:	38.7%	29.4%
No Regular Physical Activity:	52.2%	17.4%

It makes sense that health measures are heading in a downward trajectory, when the relationship between favorable amounts of physical activity and optimal health is understood.

A case in point is that the average American woman walks only about 5,100 steps per day, compared with her contemporary Amish peer who walks about 15,000 steps per day. The difference becomes more dramatic as average American women get older, with a decline to about 1,500 steps per day by the age of 60, according to findings published by *Medicine & Science in Sports & Exercise*, in October 2012[2].

[2] *Medicine & Science in Sports & Exercise:* doi: 10.1249/MSS.0b013e3181dc2e54

Another study from the University of North Carolina–Chapel Hill[3] documented and compared trends of physical activity in the U.S. and around the world. It showed that activity levels among Americans decreased by 32 percent from 1965 to 2009. By 2030, if the trend continues as expected, the decrease in activity is projected to reach 46 percent.

It's unquestionable that health measures in this country are in a negative spiral and diseases related to lifestyle choices are climbing. These trends are precipitated by physical inactivity and poor dietary habits. It doesn't matter if the root cause is technology, more leisure time, longer commutes, or anything else. What does matter is creating a culture of change to get things going in a better direction.

So, what should forward-looking women do to spearhead this change to maintain their best quality of life over the age of 50?

The answer is simple: EAT WELL AND MOVE A LITTLE MORE!

The current culture might have you think that you have to run marathons or take the grueling challenge of a cross-fit training class to see significant health results. But the truth is that moderate doses of movement and healthy eating patterns, spread throughout the course of the day, can make a huge difference in your well-being.

If you're in your 40s or 50s, it's important for you to prepare for an active retirement by taking action now. Begin by following a daily plan that starts with being mindful about your diet, in such ways as:

---

[3] Time use and physical activity: a shift away from movement across the globe
S. W. Ng, B. M. Popkin. doi: 10.1111/j.1467-789X.2011.00982.x

- **Eating well throughout the day.** Fruits and vegetables are especially beneficial because of their "anti-aging" properties.

- **Controlling portion size and not letting yourself get too hungry,** which can set the stage for poor choices and out-of-control eating.

- **Staying well-hydrated with water.** Caffeinated or sugared beverages don't fit the bill.

Then there's the daily action needed around physical activity, such as:

- **Moving more.** Take a look at your current daily activity level. Be honest with yourself. This is your starting point from which to improve. Increase your activity level week by week in moderate increments. Walk to the store, take the stairs, mow the lawn, dance in the kitchen. Look for opportunities to move and make life more physical.

- **Moving often.** Just one round per day of exercise is not enough. Weave movement into your life every chance you get. Make it a lifestyle.

- **Mixing it up.** Doing the same thing over and over isn't as beneficial as moving in many different ways. So, go for a walk to increase your number of steps per day, but dance, work in the garden, wash the car by hand, and take a Tai Chi or yoga class as well.

Retirement Plan Ahead Action Steps

Careful planning can help you achieve success on a day-to-day basis. Here are five action steps to keep you "ahead of the game."

1 Tune Into a Healthy Mind-Set

Set the stage at the beginning of each day to be very mindful of taking care of yourself.

2 Create a System of Reminders

Habits don't change without thought and care. Place sticky notes around your home, at your desk, or on the dashboard of your car to make good choices around food. Use a timer on your cell phone or Google calendar to send yourself reminders to get up and move during your day.

3 Make Friends with Other Like-Minded Women

Peer-to-peer motivation is very compelling and will help to keep you on track.

4 Remain Patient

Mindful change is a process. To change and develop new habits takes time. The likelihood of long-term success increases if you allow gradual improvements. Remove the temptation for drastic and quick change.

5 Congratulate Yourself on Your New Lifestyle!

Now that you've taken sane and sensible steps to enjoy the satisfaction and enormous health benefits of eating well and moving more, go tell your friends. Get them to join the "movement" with you. Then, all we need to do is go find Rebecca and bring her along, too.

IT'S YOUR RETIREMENT: WHAT DO YOU *REALLY* WANT IT TO BE?

BY AMY WOOD

An award-winning psychologist gives sound advice on listening to your inner compass.

Regarding intuition as a trustworthy compass for navigating our perpetually hectic age, psychologist Amy Wood guides women to their inner wisdom through therapeutic coaching, speaking, writing, and workshops. She wrote the award-winning book *Life Your Way,* is an eRelationshipAdviceCafé.com columnist, cohosts *The Leadership Lab* radio show, and is often interviewed by media ranging from local newspapers to *PARADE Magazine.* To learn more, go to amywoodpsyd.com.

HOW ARE WE DOING?

It's not your mother's retirement. Nor is it your sister's, your neighbor's, or your spouse's retirement for that matter either. What's great about planning for retirement in an era when personal reinvention is all the rage — at any age — is that the sky's the limit. Retirement has snowballed from playing cards in Florida to going back to school, starting a new career, traveling the globe, coming out, transforming your hobby into an income, saving the planet, or doing whatever else you're craving. Anything is possible, and you have complete and utter freedom to create a next stage that utterly suits you.

Of course, the catch to the "carte blanche" retirement approach is that you have to trust your inner inclinations implicitly in order to exercise all that freedom in ways that will most likely make you happy. In the face of endless next-stage options clamoring for your attention, you'll get pulled in all sorts of wrong directions if you don't have the self-knowledge necessary to define and sculpt your own path. If you expect to successfully carve out a fulfilling future for yourself from the commotion of beckoning possibilities, you must put your intuition in charge of your destiny.

> "Put your intuition in charge of your destiny."

ENCOURAGE YOUR INTUITION TO SPEAK TO YOU

Ready to leave her nursing career but not financially secure enough to stop working, Wendy had no idea what was next, until an entrepreneurship seminar unexpectedly caught her eye and ignited a passion that led her to open her own boutique. All set to move to a golf development in a warmer climate with her husband after years of careful retirement planning, Camille ended up happily divorced and living in an urban loft when a particularly vivid dream awakened her desire to live solo in a northern city. Even though moving into a splendid retirement community closer to her grandchildren made perfect sense to Tina, a lingering, uneasy "hunch" caused her to stay put in the town she loved and share a house with two close friends instead.

You're well aware as a grown woman that inner-directed decisions usually lead to resonant results like the ones above, but it's hard to hear what your all-knowing intuition has to say amid all the noise of modern life. The solution is to consciously create situations that encourage your intuition to speak to you, starting right now, no matter how far off retirement seems. If you make it a consistent practice to step away from outside distractions, pause, and listen, you'll enjoy increasingly meaningful and reassuring inner instincts that will ultimately lead you to a customized retirement that totally fits you. No matter how preoccupied you are or how long it's been since you heeded your own guidance, your intuition is right there, waiting inside you like a patient, loyal friend. All you have to do is slow down, summon your inner adviser, and give it a warm, inviting welcome. The more you exercise your intuition, the better prepared you'll be to greet retirement when the time comes.

> "Your intuition is right there, waiting inside you like a patient, loyal friend."

PAYING ATTENTION TO YOUR INNER COMPASS

Here are five steps to help you get reacquainted with your intuition:

1. Put your health first. You will hear your intuition most clearly when you are well rested and amply nourished. So get plenty of sleep, eat healthfully, drink lots of water, kick any bad habits compromising your longevity, and surround yourself with supportive people who encourage you to follow inner counsel that may make sense only to you.

2. Clear out the clutter. Intuition is not aggressive, which means you have to make space for it to be heard. Getting rid of what you no longer want or need – clothes that don't fit, stuff you don't use,

people who drag you down, beliefs that don't inspire you, obligations that drain you — encourages your inner voice to settle in and assert itself.

③ Rein in your technology use. Subtle intuitive signs and sensations can't compete with the intoxicating stimulation of whatever gadgets keep you connected to cyberspace. The Internet is infinitely useful, but only if you access it judiciously in ways that encourage rather than drown out your inner voice.

④ Take time to decide. Your intuition can be slow in surfacing, so it's important that you don't act impulsively if you want to make choices that truly satisfy. Ask yourself what you're really in the mood for before you reflexively order that same old thing at your favorite lunch place. Likewise, tell friends and colleagues asking for favors or your company that you'll get back to them after you've thought through their requests.

⑤ Break away on a regular basis. Intuition speaks most openly when you are relaxed and in the flow of the moment, not when you are beating away at a problem or forcing your way through your never-ending to-do list. Traditional meditation is an excellent exercise for encouraging impromptu intuitive hits, as is walking in nature, swimming laps, gardening, or any other appealing activity that allows your thoughts to meander.

ONE WOMAN'S VIEW
SAMANTHA'S STORY: "I have to design and implement my own retirement"

Samantha, a single advertising executive with a packed social calendar, is 43 and *well into* planning her retirement. *"I understand as an independent woman that I have to design and implement my own retirement, just like I've done with my career and my life. I'm pretty particular, and I know that the right retirement isn't going to just fall into place; I have to actively manifest what I want, and saving money is just one piece of that."* How does she find time to plan for retirement when she has so much going on right now? *"I used to be afraid that if I focused on retirement, I'd accomplish less in the present. But the more I look inside myself and discover what I want at my core, the clearer I get on my future and how to get there — and that makes my life right now a lot less stressful and way more rewarding. I get my best insights when I'm running, and I write down my retirement ideas as they occur to me. My perfect retirement is evolving over time."*

Retirement   Plan Ahead   Action Steps

1 Tap Your Intuition

Ask your intuition for a few suggestions on what you can do to move in the direction of a retirement scenario that resonates with you. What might you let go of? What might you bring in?

2 Activate Your Imagination

Gather together some old magazines, quickly leaf through them, and rip out images and words that speak to you about your dream retirement. Now make a collage, step away, and observe. What does your intuition have to say about what you see?

3 Recall Influences from Your Past to Create Your Future

Look back to passions and pastimes from your childhood. As you recall favorite books, TV shows, and movies; influential people; and goals and interests you let go of long ago for one reason or another, are there insights you have about yourself that might help you to make your retirement more rewarding?

4 Picture Your Ideal Lifestyle

Take time on a regular basis to fully envision your retirement. What will it look like, be like, feel like? How will you spend your time? What will you value most? Will you be alone or partnered? The more you can identify and rehearse the emotions associated with your dream retirement — contentment, engagement, stimulation, joy — the more likely you are to advance in line with your intuitive desires.

5 Think About What Scares You

Acknowledge any concerns and fears about retirement that are keeping you awake at night. Ask your intuition what steps you can take to feel calmer so that you can plan your next life stage from a place of faith and confidence.

PACK YOUR SPIRITUAL KNAPSACK FOR RETIREMENT

BY PAT HOERTDOERFER, M.Div.

A much-admired minister and educator reflects on the vital role of spirituality in retirement.

Rev. Patricia Hoertdoerfer is an experienced educator, Unitarian Universalist minister, and consultant. She received her B.A. and M.A. from the University of Colorado and her M.Div. from Meadville Lombard Theological School. Although currently retired from active Unitarian Universalist ministry, she served the UU Association at continental, district, and congregational levels over the past 35 years. She is active with Sage-ing® International as a Certified Sage-ing® Leader, designing programs and leading workshops, and she recently served as the 2012 International Sage-ing® Conference chairperson.

RETIREMENT REENVISIONED

In this ever-changing world, we ask: What is this transition we call "retirement" — is it retiring from adulthood to old age? Or possibly retiring from health and work to disengagement and decline? How appropriate is the term retirement for a vital person today with 30 or more years to live? Retirement as it has been commonly conceived for the past 75 years can turn purposeful lives into casualties. James Hillman in *The Force of Character* talks about "finishing" our lives, "burnishing our character to a high gloss." This model of aging requires us to develop the most authentic expression of who we are and leave a legacy for future generations. This kind of "finishing" in retirement calls for intention and engagement.

THE SPIRITUAL STAGES OF RETIREMENT

I invite you to bring a spiritual dimension into your retirement and aging. It is your choice! To me, spirituality is our relationship with the Spirit or Source of Life, whatever we understand that to be. My spirituality is my contemplative and expressed response to the wonder and joy, pain and grief of being alive. One great purpose of spirituality is to restore our connection to each other, or rather, to awaken our awareness to the connections that exist. Spirituality is our experience of being a part of a larger whole, and it can help us through the transitions that accompany retirement.

As we explore these transitions, let us remember that life is full of changes, times of holding on and letting go, times of sadness and hope. As William Bridges writes in his book *Transitions: Making Sense of Life's Changes*, transitions begin with Endings, move on into a Wilderness (or Neutral Zone), cross the Threshold from internal contemplation to external action, and then risk the creative newness of a New Beginning. Transitions are a natural process of disorientation and reorientation, marking the turning points in our path of growth. You have already lived a lifetime of transitions!

If you are contemplating retirement, or are rethinking what retirement means to you, I invite you to explore how these various transitional stages apply to retirement and how you can use some common spiritual practices to help you through them. When we embrace this encore period of our lives with hope and curiosity, courage and creativity, we must pause and revisit the same abiding questions of previous transitions: *Who am I? Where do I belong? What is my work? What is my unique gift or calling?* Wherever you are in your retirement or nonretirement transition, take time now to reflect on future possibilities with spiritual intentions and practices.

{ "How have your transitions changed your life? How have you marked major turning points in your life?" }

ENDINGS

We have to deal with endings all our lives: when we finish school, leave home, lose a loved one, recognize when a career has run its course. Yet we are not very good at this process, and in many ways our culture denies the need for endings, both personal and institutional. If we are to make a healthy transition from a rewarding career into a different kind of work in retirement, we need to pay attention to the dynamics of closure in order to make room for future growth. "Letting go" of our identity associated with our career or primary adult role is difficult, especially when leaving positions of power and influence and giving up title and salary.

In thinking about Endings in terms of transitioning into the retirement years ahead, you may struggle with how to cope with both the external and internal changes that can feel so daunting and challenging. Finding some quiet time and space in your busy life for reflection can help you keep your bearings. With times of silence and deep breathing, you can become aware of your inner life and your whole self: body, mind, heart, and soul. A regular spiritual practice of gratitude can be an important way to prepare to let go and give thanks for "what was."

Journaling reflection: gratitude

Through the spiritual practice of journal writing, you can learn to be a witness to your own experiences, recording how your life unfolds and getting in touch with your deepest feelings.

> ▶ Recall two Endings that were significant to you. What was being completed in each one? How did you acknowledge the importance of each one?

> ▶ Is there something in your work that remains unfinished? What ritual or action might help you move on?

> ▶ Each day for a week, write down five things you are grateful for that day. Examine them and explore the hopefulness that may open for you.

WILDERNESS

In Wilderness time, we are often in the dark, confused and frustrated. We aren't sure what is happening to us or how long it will go on. We don't know whether we are going crazy or becoming enlightened. Suffering the confusing nowhere of being "in between," we may miss an important self-discovery and lose the opportunity it provides for a deepened sense of purpose. In the Wilderness phase of retirement, we leave behind thoughts of a job or career and begin to consider our *vocare*, our real calling, which is an expression of who we are now and why we are here. Embracing Wilderness time means rethinking our doing, retirement or nonretirement. What is your work now?

{ *"Embracing Wilderness time means rethinking our doing."* }

Spiritual conversations

Spiritual practices such as exploring nature, making a retreat, or visualizing your future can be particularly helpful at this stage. It is an excellent time to seek a spiritual companion and engage in conversations of spiritual intimacy. The gift you give to one another is speaking with complete honesty and listening deeply.

THRESHOLD

Until this point, the phases of a retirement transition are mostly internal. Making a decision to embrace a new identity and a new vocation requires courage and hopefulness. The Threshold or crossing point between pondering and visible new beginnings is a critical time. There is help available through coaches, faith communities, and educational institutions. To assess your needs and abilities and find support, look to guidance from a spiritual community and trusted colleagues or mentors.

Intentional community

Gather your community together, form a circle, light a candle, and hold the space open for whatever is to occur in your future. Relating to others in a community of spiritual practice will help you remember that you belong to something larger than yourself.

NEW BEGINNINGS

> "The real voyage of discovery consists
> Not in seeking new landscapes
> But in having new eyes."
>
> —Marcel Proust

Our ability to risk a new venture at this stage of life depends on whether we have cultivated fear or trust in our earlier years. The way we approach creative newness and our tolerance for risk is usually cultivated at home, during childhood. When parents told stories of their early years, they passed on values even before we had the language to understand them. Our feelings about risk are also shaped by our own life experiences. As you contemplate your future retirement, do you think you'll be willing to risk stepping into a new environment and perhaps putting yourself in new work situations? By doing so, you may have opportunities to nurture neglected parts of yourself and move toward wholeness.

Stepping into New Beginnings in terms of new work is a process of letting go of your public persona and replacing it with the creative person who is at your core. Discovering the unique gift of your true self is both a risk and a blessing.

{ "Discovering the unique gift of your true self is both a risk and a blessing." }

The spiritual practice of discernment

Discernment is finding language for bringing what may have been a wordless inner experience of relationship to a larger realm of spiritual connection. Know that it is an ongoing process and one that requires discernment or listening to your deepest calling. Find a creative way to tell the story of your transition and express your new calling — draw it, sing it, write a poem, create a video.

"CALLINGS NEVER END"

Recalling my retirement transition story is essential to meeting the challenge and privilege of finishing my life well. Heeding my call, my unique gift now, I am growing and evolving to the very end of my life. As James Hillman writes in *The Force of Character*, "We may retire from a job or our career, but there is no relaxing from our individual callings. Calling not only precedes career but outlasts it as well. Callings never end when careers do. . . . No one ever becomes uncalled. Our vocational story unfolds from cradle to grave."

As I approach my mid-70s, I am deep into my calling, my ministry to and with elders. I'm going home, conscious of what I have left behind as I move forward, stripped down to my core. It's not a hero's journey but truly a human one, and I keep going with my eyes wide open, humming my song, and breathing deeply.

Retirement Plan Ahead **Action Steps**

1 Take Time for Meditation and Reflection

Meditation and reflection start with quieting your mind, breathing deeply, and opening to deeper levels of understanding. Look for moments of gratefulness; honor every voice inside of you as it emerges.

2 Write in Your Journal

Write about what is happening — what you are missing, feeling, hoping for. Your journal can include inspirational words from the world's wisdom traditions. It will help you to become better acquainted with the many parts of your Self and to explore your dreams.

3 Inventory Your Resources

Take stock of your strengths; name people to whom you can turn for emotional support. Revisit prior transitions and write down what you learned from them.

4 Make a Retreat

Get away somewhere for a silent or guided retreat. Take time to meditate and visualize your ideal outcomes. What do you want your future to look like? What will add meaning to your life?

5 Tell Your Story, Share Yourself

Write a dialogue between the "Old Me" and the "New Me" and share your story in creative ways. Be encouraged by other stories of transition and inspire others with your story.

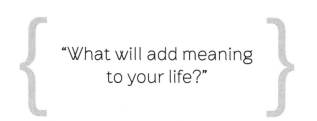

"What will add meaning to your life?"

CONTRIBUTOR BIOS (in alphabetical order)

Sally Abrahms

Sally Abrahms writes on boomer and senior housing, caregiving, and 50+ work for consumer and corporate clients. Her pieces have appeared in *TIME, Newsweek,* the *New York Times,* the *Wall Street Journal,* and *USA Today,* and on Forbes. com and *Huffington Post.* Sally blogs weekly for AARP and biweekly for Intel-GE's Care Innovations. She is the author of two books. Check out her Web site at sallyabrahms.com.

Marci Alboher

Marci Alboher is a leading authority on the changing face of work and a vice president at Encore.org, a nonprofit making it easier for millions of people to pursue second acts for the greater good.

Marci's most recent book is *The Encore Career Handbook: How to Make a Living and a Difference in the Second Half of Life,* published by Workman Publishing in 2013. She is the author of *One Person/Multiple Careers: The Original Guide to the Slash "/" Career* (originally published in 2007 and rereleased in 2012), which popularized the term "slasher" to refer to those individuals who can't answer "What do you do?" with a single word or phrase. She also created the "Shifting Careers" column and blog for the *New York Times* and the "Working the New Economy" blog for Yahoo. Her articles have appeared in scores of national publications, including *Time Out New York, Travel + Leisure, The Chronicle of Philanthropy, The International Herald Tribune,* and *More* magazine.

Marci makes frequent appearances in the media, offering advice and commentary about slashing, encore careers, and other workplace trends. She has been featured in such outlets as the *TODAY Show*, *NBC Nightly News,* and National Public Radio, as well as countless print and Web publications.

Marci is on the board of Girls Write Now, the advisory council of Echoing Green's Work on Purpose program, and the advisory board of The OpEd Project. She holds an undergraduate degree in English from the University of Pennsylvania and a law degree from the Washington College of Law at American University.

A bit of the personal: Marci grew up on the Jersey Shore, living above her family's motel, and has lived in Philadelphia, Washington, DC, and Hong Kong. She always finds her way back to New York City, where she has spent more than 15 years. In her free time, she reads, travels, walks (excessively), and plays low-stakes poker. She lives in Greenwich Village with her husband, an entrepreneur/designer, and their French bulldog, Sinatra.

Dawn Angelo

Start Now — Planning for Retirement Begins Today! 154
Dawn Angelo is the Regional CEO for the American Red Cross in Western Washington, serving 3.5 million people by providing disaster relief and community preparedness. She began her Red Cross career nearly seven years ago in Spokane, Washington, and also served as Regional CEO for the Capital Region, based in Sacramento, California.

Prior to the American Red Cross, she served as the volunteer director for Catholic Charities Minneapolis/St. Paul, an organization that engaged over 11,000 volunteers annually, and also Volunteers of America Minnesota, that sponsored a wide range of volunteer programs, including the Retired and Senior Volunteer Program (RSVP) and AmeriCorps.

As a 2000–2001 fellow for the Corporation for National and Community Service, Dawn studied new approaches to engage and recruit aging baby boomers for volunteer service, and in 2002, she studied with Dr. Margaret Wheatley to conduct research for her thesis, "Building Community through Local Leaders." She also had a lead role developing Minnesota's first-ever collaborative program on "Advocacy Leadership for Vital Aging," a certificate program through the University of Minnesota–College of Continuing Education.

Dawn has always volunteered through a variety of roles, including mediator, teacher, neighborhood leader, neighborhood board member, trainer, and consultant. Most recently, she joined the Literacy Council of Seattle board. She can be reached at: www.linkedin.com/pub/dawn-lindblom-angelo/1/184/316/.

Nancy Collamer, M.S.

How to Reinvent Your Career for Semi-Retirement 94

Nancy Collamer is an author, career coach, speaker, and recognized expert on second-act careers, semi-retirement, and boomer career trends. She writes a semimonthly career blog for the PBS Web site NextAvenue.org and Forbes.com. She is the author of *Second-Act Careers: 50+ Ways to Profit from Your Passions During Semi-Retirement* (Ten Speed Press, 2013), and was a featured contributor in *65 Things to Do When You Retire* (Sellers Publishing, Inc., 2012).

Forbes named Nancy's Web site, MyLifestyleCareer.com, as one of the "Top 100 Web Sites for Your Career" in both 2012 and 2013.

In private practice since 1996, Nancy holds an M.S. in career development from the College of New Rochelle and a B.A. in psychology from the University of North Carolina at Chapel Hill. Her advice has been featured in numerous media outlets, including *NBC Nightly News*, the *New York Times*, CNN, the *Wall Street Journal*, *Redbook*, *Ladies' Home Journal*, *More*, *Fortune*, and *O, The Oprah Magazine*. She has written columns about lifestyle-friendly careers for a number of major Web sites, including

Forbes.com, AARP.org, NextAvenue.org, and Job-Hunt.org. Nancy enjoys sharing her expertise with live audiences, both large and small, and has spoken at venues ranging from Harvard Business School to the California Governor & First Lady's Conference on Women. You can connect with Nancy on her Web site at mylifestylecareer.com or on Twitter @NancyCollamer.

Sara Zeff Geber, Ph.D. CRC

Dr. Sara Zeff Geber is a speaker, writer, workshop leader, and certified retirement and transition coach. She is the founder of LifeEncore, a coaching and consulting business, and is an expert in retirement transition for baby boomers. She is on the national board of the Life Planning Network (LPN) and is the program chair for the Northern California Chapter. Sara is also a sponsor and partner of the Silicon Valley chapter of the Financial Planning Association.

Sara conducts retirement-transition workshops for industry and government, and is a sought-after speaker in the San Francisco Bay Area with her talks "Eight Keys to a Successful Retirement," "The Boomer Retirement Dilemma," and "Fifty Plus, Minus Kids."

Sara's specialty within the life-planning arena is working with couples and singles without children. Sara envisions this group having unique needs in later life that warrant additional consideration and planning. She has been researching, speaking, and writing about this topic for over two years.

Sara has a Ph.D. in counseling and organizational behavior, an M.A. in guidance and counseling, and a B.A in psychology. She is a coauthor of *Live Smart After 50!*, a 2013 LPN publication; the author of *How to Manage Stress for Success*, an AMACOM WorkSmart Series book; and a chapter author of "Choices," in *GPS for Success*. In connection with her previous work as an organizational consultant and leadership coach, Sara has spoken at a variety of conferences and symposia, including "Aging in America" (the annual American Society for Aging conference and expo, 2013), the "Positive Aging Conference" (2010 and 2011), and the "Vital Aging Conference" (2011). She has also spoken at the Academy of Management, and at the American Society for Training and Development. Most recently, she was a featured speaker at the Palo Alto Medical Foundation's highly acclaimed "Successful Aging" symposium and expo.

Sara is married and makes her home in Los Gatos, California.

Pat Hoertdoerfer, M.Div.

Rev. Patricia Hoertdoerfer is an experienced educator, Unitarian Universalist minister, and consultant. She received her B.A. and M.A. from the University of Colorado and her M. Div. from Meadville Lombard Theological School. Although currently retired from active Unitarian Universalist ministry, she served the UU Association at continental, district, and congregational levels over the past 35 years. In her curriculum-development work, she published multigenerational resources, including an *Elderhood and Spirituality Reflection and Discussion Guide to Zalman Schachter-Shalomi's book, From Age-ing to Sage-ing*. She has shared her leadership experience in academic institutions, community organizations, and interfaith communities. In retirement, she is active with Sage-ing® International as a Certified Sage-ing® Leader, designing programs and leading workshops, and in 2012 she served as the International Sage-ing® Conference chairperson.

M. Cindy Hounsell

M. Cindy Hounsell is the President of WISER, the Women's Institute for a Secure Retirement, a nonprofit organization that seeks to improve the opportunities for women to secure retirement income and to educate the public about the inequities that disadvantage women in retirement.

An attorney and retirement expert, she has been widely quoted in the *New York Times, Washington Post, Los Angeles Times, Boston Globe, Christian Science Monitor, USA Today, Newsweek, Barrons, Investor's Business Daily, Congressional Quarterly, Ms., Working Mother,* Associated Press, Knight Ridder, and Reuters. She has appeared on ABC, CBS, CNN, CNBC, Fox Morning News & Financial News, and a *Good Morning America* interview with Diane Sawyer. The PBS program *To the Contrary* filmed a two-part award-winning series on women and retirement that featured WISER. Radio interviews include several syndicated shows, such as National Public Radio's *All Things Considered* and *Marketplace.*

Cindy has testified before Congress, and has served as a delegate for a number of White House Summits and conferences, including the last two White House Conferences on Aging, the White House Social Security Conference, and each of the National Retirement Saver Summits. She has written several chapters, columns, articles, op-eds, papers, and booklets on women and retirement. Two booklets, *What Every WOMAN Needs to Know About MONEY and RETIREMENT: A Simple Guide* and *What Everyone Needs to Know About Money and Retirement,* appeared as inserts in *Good Housekeeping* magazine, to an audience of over 26 million readers.

Cindy provides technical assistance to several national organizations, as well as training to leaders and grassroots advocates around the country, as part of her role as director of the National Education and Resource Center on Women and Retirement Planning, funded by the U.S. Administration on Aging.

Cindy was appointed in 2011 by Secretary of Labor Hilda Solis to the ERISA Advisory Council, and in 2008 by the Bush Administration to the Advisory Panel on Medicare Education

(APME), representing the field of retirement and financial planning. She serves on the boards of the National Alliance for Caregiving and STRIVE DC, and on the Advisory Council of Wider Opportunities for Women's Elder Economic Security Initiative and the Financial Services Roundtable's Retirement Advisory Council. She is also a member of the National Academy of Social Insurance. In 2012, *Money Magazine* named Cindy Hounsell one of their "Money Heroes" as part of a year-long celebration of 40 people who have made extraordinary efforts to improve the financial well-being of others. *Women's eNews* also honored her as one of *21 Leaders for the 21st Century.* Finally, the National Adult Protective Services Association recently recognized Cindy for her leadership and commitment to older women by presenting her with their NAPSA Collaboration Award.

Julie Jason

Over the last 20 years, money manager and lawyer Julie Jason has established herself as an expert in retirement investing, a special focus of her firm, Jackson, Grant Investment Advisers, Inc., of Stamford, Connecticut. She is the author of two highly acclaimed books on the subject, *The AARP® Retirement Survival Guide* and *Managing Retirement Wealth*, both winners of the prestigious EIFLE Award for Excellence in Financial Literacy Education. Her award-winning investor-education column is syndicated by King Features. You can write to Julie at readers@juliejason.com or visit her Web sites: juliejason.com and jacksongrantus.com.

Akaisha Kaderli

Having retired at the age of 38 in 1991, Akaisha Kaderli and her husband, Billy, are recognized retirement experts and internationally published authors on topics of finance, world travel, and medical tourism. They have been interviewed about retirement issues by the *Wall Street Journal, Kiplinger's Personal Finance Magazine, The Motley Fool Rule Your Retirement* newsletter, nationally syndicated radio talk-show host Clark Howard, Bankrate.com, *SmartMoney, Minyanville, FOXBusiness,* and countless newspapers and TV shows nationally and worldwide.

With the wealth of information they share on their popular Web site, RetireEarlyLifestyle.com, they have been helping people achieve their own retirement dreams since 1991. Continuing to journal and photograph their world travels, Billy and Akaisha have home bases in Thailand, Mexico, Guatemala, and the U.S. They have been married over three decades, and enjoy the world of finance, fine cuisine, photography, publishing, playing tennis, volunteering, traveling, and learning about native peoples.

Moira Lanier

Moira Lanier is the founder, president, chief motivator, and head trainer of Greatest Age Fitness, Inc., a unique physical-training center for people over the age of 50 or those who want to have a head start on getting in shape for their later years. Her philosophy is to provide age-appropriate instruction, coaching, and support in a setting where people treat their bodies mindfully and respectfully in the face of aging. Moira's center is located in West Newton, Massachusetts. She is also a contributing author to *Live Smart After 50! The Experts' Guide to Life Planning for Uncertain Times* and a member of the Life Planning Network.

Suzanne Braun Levine

Inventing Your Best Retirement . . . A Circle of Trust Is a Must 78
Suzanne Braun Levine is a writer, editor, and authority on women, families, media, and changing gender roles. She was the first editor of *Ms.* magazine and the first woman editor of the *Columbia Journalism Review*. She reports on the changes in women's lives in her books, on her Web site, on television and radio, and as a blogger for AARP, Huff/Post 50, Next Avenue, Feminist.com, and others. She is on the board of Encore.org and the Ms. Foundation for Education and Communication, Inc., on the advisory board for the Women's Media Center and The Transition Network, and is a contributing editor at *More* magazine.

She is the author of the e-book *You Gotta Have Girlfriends: A Post-Fifty Posse Is Good for Your Health* (2013/Open Road Media). It is a continuation of her ongoing conversation with women in second adulthood, the new stage of life she celebrated in her popular books *Inventing the Rest of Our Lives, Fifty Is the New Fifty,* and *How We Love Now.* Her new e-book, *Can Men Have It All?* and *What "The Daddy Track" Means for Women* (2014/ Shebooks), examines the changing role of fatherhood and the state of work-life trade-offs for modern couples, topics she introduced in her pioneering book, *Father Courage* (2000).

In 2007, she coauthored (with Mary Thom) a widely acclaimed oral history of New York Congresswoman Bella Abzug. While at *Ms.,* she developed, conceived, and produced the Peabody Award–winning HBO special *She's Nobody's Baby: American Women in the 20th Century,* and edited the book based on the documentary. She was editor-in-chief of the 30th anniversary issue of *Ms.* and was honored as a *"Ms.* Woman of the Year" in 2004.

She graduated with honors from Harvard University and has taught journalism at several universities. Suzanne lives in New York with her husband, Robert F. Levine, an attorney. They have two adult children. Her Web site is suzannebraunlevine.com.

Kali Lightfoot

Kali Lightfoot is executive director of the National Resource Center for Osher Lifelong Learning Institutes (OLLIs). She holds a B.A. from Western Michigan University and an M.S. from the University of Washington. Kali was on the management staff at Elderhostel (now known as Road Scholar) for over 20 years, holding program positions in the domestic, international, and service-learning divisions. She has also taught in high school and college, served as director of International Elder Programs for the Experiment in International Living, and worked as a wilderness ranger for the U.S. Forest Service. Kali was director of the Senior College at University of Southern Maine (USM), which later became the first OLLI. In 2004, USM was chosen by the Osher Foundation to create and manage the National Resource Center for the OLLIs, with Kali as its founding director. She is a graduate of Leadership Maine, and past chair of the Lifetime Education and Renewal Network of the American Society on Aging. She is a member of the Health, Physical Education, and Recreation Alumni Honor Academy at WMU, and was awarded the Golden Apple by the alumni of the WMU College of Education. Kali is currently studying for an M.F.A. in Poetry at Vermont College of Fine Arts.

Kathryn McCamant

Kathryn McCamant, a licensed architect, is coauthor of the book *Cohousing: A Contemporary Approach to Housing Ourselves,* which introduced this European housing model to North America. In 1987, Kathryn and her husband, Chuck Durrett, founded McCamant & Durrett Architects. In 2006, she founded CoHousing Partners, a cohousing development firm, with Jim Leach. Over the last two decades, Kathryn has designed, developed, and consulted on over 50 cohousing communities in the U.S., as well as working with communities internationally. She has worked in every phase of cohousing development, from site search to construction administration, from marketing and outreach to living in her own communities. In 2011, Chuck and Kathryn released *Creating Cohousing: Building Sustainable Communities* (New Society Press), which covers their 20 years of creating cohousing communities across North America. She is now utilizing her experience to work with groups and developers across the country to assist them in creating their own communities. Her work has received numerous national awards. Kathryn often lectures and offers workshops for people interested in creating more community in their lives. After living in the very urban Doyle Street Cohousing in Emeryville for 12 years, she now lives in Nevada City Cohousing in the California Sierra Foothills. www.cohousingpartners.com; www.mccamant-durrett.com.

Dorian Mintzer, M.S.W., Ph.D., BCC

Dorian Mintzer is a licensed psychologist, career/life-transition coach, money and relationship coach, executive coach, speaker, writer, consultant, and teacher. With over 40 years of clinical experience, she is a licensed third-age coach, a 2Young2Retire certified facilitator, a licensed life-change artist, and a licensed paper-room coach-facilitator. She facilitates workshops and speaks to community, corporate, and professional groups on topics related to midlife and second-half-of-life issues.

Dorian is a member of a number of professional organizations, which include the National Speaker's Association and The Life Planning Network. She is founder of the Boomers and Beyond Special Interest Group for Interdisciplinary Professionals, which began in May 2007, and the Fourth Tuesday Retirement Interview Series for professionals and the public, which began in May 2012.

She utilizes her life experiences and expertise in adult development, positive psychology, and holistic life planning in her work with helping individuals and couples navigate the second half of life. She is coauthor of *The Couple's Retirement Puzzle*, and is a contributing author to *70 Things to Do When You Turn 70*, *Six Secrets to a Happy Retirement*, *65 Things to Do When You Retire: Travel*, *Live Smart After 50!*, *65 Things to Do When You Retire, Remarkable and Real!*, and *Making Marriage a Success*. She has been quoted in a number of publications, such as the *Wall Street Journal*, the *New York Times*, *USA Today*, *CNN Money*, NPR's *Talk of the Nation*, and the *ABC Evening News* with Diane Sawyer. You can learn more about Dorian at revolutionizeretirement.com.

Nancy Merz Nordstrom

Nancy Merz Nordstrom is the author of *Learning Later, Living Greater: The Secret for Making the Most of Your After-50 Years* (2006, Sentient Publications, Boulder, Colorado), which introduces readers to the ideas and benefits of later-life learning. It challenges people to become involved in meaningful new avenues of productivity: learning for the sheer joy of learning something new, educational travel, volunteerism, civic action, and more. It shows them how to stay mentally and spiritually young. *Learning Later, Living Greater* is the guidebook for transforming the after-work years into a richly satisfying period of personal growth and social involvement.

Nancy also directs a national network of over 400 noncredit lifelong-learning programs for older adults on college and university campuses, and in other venues, across the United States and Canada. She has given presentations, workshops, and courses that speak to later-life enrichment and satisfaction, using the tools of learning, exploring, and serving. As an expert, she has also been interviewed by scholars, writers, and the media (newspapers, radio, and TV) about the concept, benefits, and opportunities of lifelong learning for older adults.

Elizabeth O'Brien

Elizabeth O'Brien writes the "Retire Well" column for the *Wall Street Journal*'s MarketWatch.com, covering the intersection of health and wealth in retirement planning. She earned a B.A. in comparative literature from Brown University and an M.S. in journalism from Columbia University. Elizabeth lives with her husband and two young sons in Brooklyn, New York, where she tries to turn every playground visit into a workout.

Shirley Sagawa

Shirley Sagawa, cofounder of the sagawa/jospin consulting firm, was named a "Woman to Watch in the 21st Century" by *Newsweek* magazine, and one of the "Most Influential Working Mothers in America" by *Working Mother* magazine. She is currently a fellow with the Center for American Progress and author of *The American Way to Change* (Jossey-Bass, 2010), which describes how volunteer and national service can be a breakthrough strategy for change.

Her book with Deb Jospin, *The Charismatic Organization* (Jossey-Bass, 2008), offers breakthrough insights into building strong, effective, and well-resourced nonprofit organizations. Her previous book, *Common Interest, Common Good: Creating Value through Business and Social Sector Partnerships* (Harvard Business School Press, 1999), describes how business and social-sector organizations can collaborate for mutual gain.

Shirley has served as a presidential appointee in both the first Bush and Clinton administrations. As Deputy Chief of Staff to First Lady Hillary Clinton, she advised the First Lady on domestic policy. Shirley was instrumental to the drafting and passage of legislation creating the Corporation for National Service and AmeriCorps. After Senate confirmation as the Corporation's first chief operating and policy officer, she led the development of new service programs for adults and students, including AmeriCorps, and directed strategic planning for this new government corporation.

Shirley is a graduate of Smith College, the London School of Economics, and Harvard Law School, where she served on the *Harvard Law Review*.

Paula Solomon, MSSS

Paula Solomon is a midlife coach, presenter, workshop leader, and writer with The Seasons of Your Life Coaching. She helps women navigating midlife, who are asking "What's next?" to create intentional plans for the next season of their lives. Clients may be dreaming of work that better suits them; facing an empty nest, new caregiving responsibilities, or other life changes; or desiring a personalized "retirement." They seek a better quality of daily life.

Paula has helped clients improve their lives for over 25 years as a life coach, psychotherapist, and employee-assistance professional, and she has given presentations and workshops on a wide range of topics. Paula's personal strengths of creative perspective, big-picture thinking, practicality, and the ability to empathically relate to people enhance her work. She teaches fellow life coaches about "Well-Being in Midlife and Beyond" in the MentorCoach wellness-coaching program and is a contributor to the book *Live Smart After 50!: The Experts' Guide to Life Planning for Uncertain Times*.

Paula has served on the board of the Life Planning Network and is an affiliate of The Coaches Studio, which utilizes a research-tested model that enhances the creative process and develops important skills for successful life change.

Nancy Thompson
Nancy Thompson is an aspiring world traveler with a newly
retired spouse. A late bloomer, Nancy became a certified
personal fitness trainer at 58, and focused on fitness for
mature women. At 60, she was inspired to create Flourish,
where she produced a series of monthly salons and events to
connect, inspire, and empower women at midlife and beyond.
When Nancy and her husband hatched their plan to become
citizens of the world in retirement, she knew they were not
only going to survive but thrive. Today, she is a travel writer
and lifestyle blogger, sharing the adventures of retirement,
shoestring travel, and living the good life in retirement. Join
the adventure at justabackpackandarollie.com.

Amy Wood
Regarding intuition as a trustworthy compass for navigating
our perpetually hectic age, psychologist Amy Wood guides
women to their inner wisdom through therapeutic coaching,
speaking, writing, and workshops. She wrote the award-
winning book *Life Your Way,* is an eRelationshipAdviceCafe.com
columnist, cohosts *The Leadership Lab* radio show, and is often
interviewed by media ranging from local newspapers to
PARADE Magazine. Amy cofacilitates the day-long retirement-
planning workshop "Innovative Retirement." To learn more, go
to amywoodpsyd.com.

About the Editor

Mark Evan Chimsky is the head of Mark Chimsky Editorial Services Unlimited, an editorial consulting business based in Portland, Maine. For nearly six years, he was the editor in chief of the book division of Sellers Publishing, an independent publishing company based in South Portland, Maine. Previously he was executive editor and editorial director of Harper San Francisco and headed the paperback divisions at Little, Brown and Macmillan. In addition, he was on the faculty of New York University's Center for Publishing, and for three years he served as the director of the book section of NYU's Summer Publishing Institute. He has edited a number of best-selling books, including Johnny Cash's memoir, *Cash*, and he has worked with such notable authors as Melody Beattie, Arthur Hertzberg, Beryl Bender Birch, and Robert Coles. He was also project manager on Billy Graham's *New York Times* best-selling memoir, *Just As I Am*. He conceived of the long-running series *The Best American Erotica*, which was compiled by Susie Bright, and he was the first editor to reissue the works of celebrated novelist Dawn Powell. His editorial achievements have been noted in *Vanity Fair,* the *Nation,* and *Publishers Weekly*. He is an award-winning poet whose poetry and essays have appeared in *JAMA* (the *Journal of the American Medical Association*), *Wild Violet, Three Rivers Poetry Journal*, and *Mississippi Review*. For Sellers Publishing, he has developed and compiled a number of acclaimed books, including *Creating a Life You'll Love,* which won the silver in *ForeWord*'s 2009 Book of the Year Awards (self-help category), *65 Things to Do When You Retire,* which the *Wall Street Journal* called "[one] of the year's best guides to later life," *65 Things to Do When You Retire: Travel,* and *70 Things to Do When You Turn 70.*

CREDITS